Rx
FOR THE
soul

Rx FOR THE soul

DAVID B.
WILHELM, M.D.

OLIVER
NELSON

THOMAS NELSON PUBLISHERS
Nashville • Atlanta • London • Vancouver

Published in Nashville, Tennessee, by Thomas Nelson,
Inc., Publishers, and distributed in Canada by Word
Communications, Ltd., Richmond, British Columbia.

The Bible version used in this publication is THE NEW
KING JAMES VERSION. Copyright © 1979, 1980, 1982,
Thomas Nelson, Inc., Publishers.

Library of Congress Cataloging-in-Publication Data

Wilhelm, David B.

Rx for the soul : moments from a physician's practice
that bring inspiration and encouragement / David B.
Wilhelm.

    p.   cm.

ISBN 0-7852-7245-3 (pbk.)

   1. Christian life. 2. Medicine—Religious aspects—
Christianity. I. Title.

BV4501.2.W51975 1997

242'.4—dc21

96–40023

CIP

Printed in the United States of America.

1 2 3 4 5 6 QPK 02 01 00 99 98 97

CONTENTS

ACKNOWLEDGMENTS

With great love and devotion this book is dedicated to my wife, Deb, and my children, Lindsay and Christopher. Without your patience and unfailing support I could never have had the strength or the courage to complete such a project.

Also to my parents, Jack and Mary Alice, for showing me God in your lives and for instilling in me the belief that nothing is impossible.

Special thanks to Bruce Akin for your help and encouragement. Without your efforts this would not have become a reality.

May the glory of this book be given to my Lord, Jesus Christ. Let us never forget that only through His sacrifice do our lives have meaning, and only at the foot of the cross can hope be found.

INTRODUCTION

I plopped the heavy folder onto my friend's desk and waited for his response. His first reaction was to push his chair back a few inches. I knew what he was thinking: *Just what I need, another favor for a friend.*

"What's this?" he asked.

"Remember that book I've been telling you I was going to write?"

"Sure, I remember," he replied. "Don't tell me . . ."

"Yep, this is it. I'd appreciate it if you would take a look at it when you get a minute. I'm really interested in getting your input."

I felt a great sense of anticipation as I left the manuscript with my friend. I knew his opinion was respected in the religious community as well as in publishing circles. He knew I valued his thoughts. I couldn't help thinking, *I just hope he doesn't tell me he hates it.*

The next morning I called him bright and early. I didn't know if he'd even opened the folder yet, but I couldn't stand it any longer.

"Yes, I looked at it," he said. "As a matter of fact, I read the whole thing last night. I think you've got something good here. I guess it's true what they say."

"What's that?" I asked.

"It's impossible *not* to tell your story."

He went on to explain how he'd come to understand that everyone has a story to tell. For some, it's a story of heartache. For others, it's a story of joy and celebration. But we all have a story, a reflection of our soul.

My story evolved over a number of years. Being a physician provides numerous opportunities to ponder the deeper meanings of life. It offers many occasions to observe people at their very best and, occasionally, at their very worst. I have seen the first breath of many an infant just delivered from the mother's womb. I have seen the last breath of numerous aging souls as they prepared to leave this earth. I have delivered the message of comfort from a series of negative test results, and I have brought the devastating news that all hope is lost. I have seen aching bodies that clung desperately to life until they could do so no longer, and others that have welcomed death with open arms. Through it all, I have seen one constant: the innate desire, placed deep within the human heart, to know God. It is evidence that each of us has the need to be at peace with the Creator.

This constant inspired me to write this book. As

you read these stories, you will see the lives of some who have cherished their close relationship with the Father for many years. You will see others who are just beginning to build that bond. You will see still others who searched for the peace that such a relationship can provide but fell short. My sincere hope is that as you journey through these pages, you will be inspired to search for a greater knowledge of God. May you know the joy of answering that call from within, and in so doing, discover one of the great comforts of life. May you discover that He is your constant as well.

Chapter 1

TELL HIM WHERE
IT HURTS

We had been working with her for more than an hour, but nothing had helped. Still no pulse, no blood pressure, and no spontaneous respirations. We all knew she was dead, but it was my call, and the nurses were waiting for me to make it. I looked down at the blood on my shoes and silently wondered what I was doing there. I didn't have to be there, but I needed the money, so I agreed to work a shift in a rural emergency department.

It was supposed to be a very quiet experience, at least according to my friend who talked me into it. "You'll see a few sore throats," he said, "a couple of colds, maybe a sprained ankle or two, but nothing too complicated ever comes in over there." Sound too good to be true? It was. And I had already been through a trying day at the clinic.

I drove two hours through wind and rain to reach my destination, only to find Grandma (that's what everyone called her) waiting for me in room one. The red flannel nightgown she was wearing indicated that she had other plans for the evening. Clearly, she never anticipated ending up in the emergency room. The nurses said she had seen her local doctor only that morning complaining of chest pain, shortness of breath, and fatigue. He had recommended admission to the hospital for further testing, but she had declined. She said she was too busy and wanted to think about it for a while. She should have listened to him; it might have saved her life. She had returned home and suffered a massive heart attack. Now, I know the term *massive* isn't a medical term, but it's used quite often because it sounds so impressive. That's exactly what Grandma's heart attack had been—impressive, massive, lethal.

She had barely gotten the words out of her mouth, telling me about the crushing chest pain, when her eyes rolled backward rapidly, and the cardiac monitor's alarm sounded as she took her last spontaneous breath. The nurse beside me screamed "Code Blue," grabbed the respiratory bag, and began pumping air into the woman's lungs. I scrambled for an endotracheal tube, held it firmly in my hands, and steadied myself at the head of her bed. I knew I had to place the tube quickly; each second without oxygen greatly decreased her chances for survival. I hurriedly brushed a suction device through her mouth and throat, hoping to improve my visualization of the vocal cords, but still could see very little. I made my first quick pass with the tube, and I was in. The brisk mechanical ventilations quickly returned her ashen skin to a glowing pink.

My focus turned to her damaged heart, but the outlook wasn't good. The abnormal rhythm I had seen moments before had deteriorated to no rhythm at all, and despite receiving full CPR, she had only a faint pulse. I reached for the electrical paddles and nodded for everyone to stand clear. The first shock did nothing to restore her rhythm or her pulse, but I was not ready to give up. Three more shocks rapidly followed, steadily raising my own heart rate but, unfortunately, having no effect on hers. Over the next half hour I emptied the code cart of every medicine that could have been even remotely effective before I finally faced the facts. The woman was gone, and she wasn't coming back.

As I looked at the cold, lifeless body lying before me on the E.R. stretcher, I realized she would get no second chance. "Let's stop," I said. "Thank you for your help. Would someone please record the time?" The nurse scribbled "7:40 P.M." on the code sheet, then turned to inform me that the family had gathered in the conference room. They were anxiously awaiting my arrival.

That was the part of the job I hated the most. It's never easy to tell a family that a loved one has just departed this world. No description of the events ever seems adequate, no consolation ever appropriate.

The room was full of family members, all of whom jumped to their feet as I entered, but a heavyset, dark-haired woman in the corner immediately caught my eye. She appeared to be in charge of the gathering. I sensed that, ultimately, I would have to explain things to her satisfaction, so I took a deep breath, gathered my courage, and went right for her. I didn't know exactly what I would say, but I had learned in such situations to get right to the point.

"I'm terribly sorry," I said. "We did everything we could, but we couldn't save her. She died a few moments ago."

Looks of optimism quickly changed to grief, tears erupted, and they collapsed together on an old vinyl sofa as they tried to absorb what I had just told them. Working in the E.R. provides frequent reminders that death is an ugly visitor. I stayed with the family for a few more minutes, trying to provide comfort as best I could, then turned to leave to take care of other patients.

Before I could make my exit, a young boy, maybe ten years of age, stopped me. He held my arm, looked up at me through his tears, and asked, "Doctor, why did God have to take my grandma?"

Children can sometimes ask the most difficult questions, can't they? I stood there fully prepared to explain the pathophysiology of her heart attack or the ill effects of prolonged hypoxemia on the human brain, but his question was one I couldn't answer.

"I don't know, son, but I sure am sorry," I replied.

I entered room two with his question still rebounding in my brain. Room two contained a young woman with a complex compound fracture of her ankle. The portion of bone protruding through the skin provided my first clue that her injury would require one of the more difficult tasks in medicine: locating an orthopedic surgeon after hours in a small town.

That task completed, I moved on to the next room. Room three contained a delightful individual possessing the unmistakable bouquet of cheap hair cream, stale cigarette smoke, and three-day-old bourbon. He was no stranger to the staff in the E.R. He was, however, irate about the length of time he had been waiting to see me. I recognized him as the man who had come to the door while we were coding Grandma, asking if I knew how much longer it might take. His charming disposition was further apparent as he proceeded to tell me the exact name of the pain medication and cough syrup that he felt would best alleviate his symptoms. He seemed perturbed that something as trivial as a medical degree separated him from the prescriptions he knew he needed. He left unhappy, without them.

I proceeded to room four. Room four would prove to be a real challenge, not in the sense that it required great medical skill or quick intuitive diagnostic ability, but a challenge, to be sure. It was a swift kick in the emotions. A reality check. A tug at the heart. Before we enter room four, let me give you a little background information. When I entered medical school, I was fairly certain that a career in pediatrics lay ahead of me. After all, I loved children, they loved me as far as I could tell, and it seemed to be a logical decision. But as a third-year medical student, my perspective quickly changed. I learned that children weren't nearly as much fun to be around when they were sick as they were when they were well. They also didn't seem to like me nearly as much while I was probing, poking, and injecting them. After several weeks, the luster faded, and I soon changed direction to adult medicine.

That's what made the encounter in room four so difficult. Room four contained six-year-old Steven. He had sandy brown hair, big blue eyes, and a face that could melt your heart. Yet despite his seemingly normal outward appearance, Steven was in pain. Not just physical pain, mind you. No, Steven's pain went much deeper than his physical wounds. Steven was an abused child. His eyes were troubled, and his face revealed a knowledge of things that a six-year-old ought not know. He had multiple bruises on his face and head from a "fall" he had suffered earlier that day. At least that was the story from his mother. He also had about fifteen small circular burns on his chest, arms, and abdomen, and they were in various stages of healing. Those burns occur when the soft skin of a child comes into contact with the business end of a lit cigarette.

I asked Steven how it happened, but he turned away, refusing to answer me. I didn't take it personally, though. His behavior was understandable. After all, when you've seen the things Steven has seen, you learn to dispense trust very carefully.

The social worker interrupted our conversation: "Steven, this man is a doctor. Tell him where it hurts." Again, no response. Her gruff tone failed to penetrate even the most superficial layers of Steven's defenses. Still, I sensed that Steven wanted to trust me. He wanted to trust *anyone*. He just wasn't sure how to do that, and who could blame him? His track record with adults hadn't been that great over the last couple of years.

In the next few minutes, however, he began to open up. We talked, we joked, and he even smiled a couple of times. A wave of sadness came over me as I realized I was looking into a young pair of eyes longing for love, for acceptance, for peace. I hoped someday he would find all three. I took extra care that night as I attended to Steven and tried to assure him that we would do all we could to keep him from being hurt anymore. I knew the small physical wounds would soon be gone. The deep emotional wounds would heal much more slowly.

Steven thanked me for my help, then said his prayers before he drifted off to sleep. He prayed for his older brother and sister. He prayed for his dog. Then he prayed that his mommy and daddy would love him, that they wouldn't be so mad at him anymore. I had to leave after that.

As I sat to document my physical exam, I wondered how many Stevens are out there, silently suffering, thinking their pain is a normal part of growing up. I'd palpated the bruises on his cheeks and looked at the face of the brave young man with an uncertain future. While other children his age would be enjoying baseball games and birthday parties, Steven would be dealing with court dates and foster homes. I left the room, feeling I had done my best to help the little fellow, to minimize his pain, to ease his suffering.

I said a prayer of my own that night for Steven, asking that he could someday shed the scars of a painful childhood, that he could learn of love the way it was meant to be, that he could someday have a caring family with loving parents. I hoped the experience in the hospital hadn't been too traumatic for him. I hoped that if he remembered anything about the night, it would be the words from the social worker: her advice to open up, to turn his troubles over to someone else. And finally, I hoped he would continue to talk with the only Physician who could really help him, the One who loved him unconditionally, the One whose promises he could believe without fail. I hoped he would never be afraid to trust *Him* and tell Him where it hurts.

Chapter 2

WHY NOT ME?

Not another consult. It couldn't be. I looked in dismay at the number displayed on my little electronic intruder. *This day is supposed to be over,* I thought to myself. It was almost five o'clock in the afternoon. I had made rounds, seen patients, and done dictations. I was supposed to be going home to a nice dinner and some quality family time. But that was not to be.

The charge clerk could give me few details. It was a consult for medical management of an accident victim in the E.R. I got in my car and drove to the hospital feeling more than a little sorry for myself. After all, it had been a rough day: several work-ins at the office, an angry patient who was dissatisfied about our billing procedures, an air conditioner breakdown, and now a five o'clock consult. *Can my life get any more difficult?* I wondered.

It's funny how the providence of God works. I

needed the consult not from a medical standpoint, but from a human standpoint. I needed to meet Ray.

Have you ever heard the old saying, "No good deed goes unpunished"? I had never believed it, but if anybody ever had a right to, it would have been Ray. Ray was such a nice person that his generosity to others indirectly led to his hospitalization. He got off work that afternoon from his job as a security guard and started for home. His trip was interrupted, however, when he spotted some stranded motorists. Most of us could have probably driven by in good conscience without a second thought: "I'd like to help, but it's just too risky. You can't take any chances these days." But those weren't Ray's thoughts. No, Ray stopped to help.

Knowing little about cars, Ray decided to help the older couple push the vehicle into a vacant lot until they could call for help, but things didn't work out exactly as he planned. As he was walking back to his vehicle, another car topped the hill. Unfortunately, the driver didn't see Ray in time. Ray tried to move to escape the oncoming disaster, but the car swerved right into him. The couple said it was a terrible sight as they watched Ray's limp body being thrown more than forty feet into the air. Ray hit the pavement with enough force to knock him unconscious, loosen a few teeth, and shatter most of the bones in his upper extremities. His right foot was also seriously injured and bled profusely. Fortunately for Ray, he had no recollection of the events. He said he didn't hear a thing until the helicopter arrived.

Ray's evaluation and his preparation for surgery were already under way when I arrived in the E.R. Both arms were broken, badly bruised, and bleeding. I knew immediately that the damage to his right foot was so severe that it would never be saved. Further examination showed that blood was oozing from a large laceration on his chin and several other scrapes on his swollen, battered face. Multiple abrasions were scattered over his chest and back, but I could find no other major injury.

I helped cut away his blood-soaked jeans, only to find countless pieces of tar and gravel imbedded in his thighs, "road rash" as we called it in the E.R. Some of the more superficial fragments came out easily. The deeper ones were left behind for removal during surgery. I tried to be as upbeat as possible in talking to Ray, but the pain medication I had ordered had taken effect, and he was drifting in and out of awareness.

Ray would later remark that the pain wasn't really all that bad, but the surgery was. Ray's attempt at being a good Samaritan had landed him in the midst of a major operation to remove his right foot and repair both of his badly injured arms. It seemed so unjust. But Ray was still alive, and he would soon be very thankful for that.

Hours later I stood at Ray's bedside in the recovery room and assessed his overall condition. He began to awaken as the anesthesia cleared from his system, but still he could see nothing. His face was so badly injured that his eyes were bruised and swollen completely shut. It would be another two days before he was able to see that his foot, the portion of his body that was so painful to him, was actually no longer there.

I wondered how he could recover from such an accident. Life would be so different without the full use of his legs. I questioned which would be worse: Would it be the obvious physical pain that he would have to endure? Or would it be the gradual emotional strain that would grind at the psyche, insidiously taking its toll? I realized both would be formidable opponents to conquer.

During the course of Ray's hospitalization, I got to know him pretty well. He came through the postoperative period without incident, tolerated his medications without complaint, and seemed to try very hard in physical therapy. I was very pleased with his progress, but his attitude impressed me most. It was remarkable. Ray seemed happy. Occasionally, he was singing as I entered the room. I couldn't understand how he managed to be coping so well. Yet he was indeed doing well. From a medical standpoint I knew I had done all I could for Ray. I knew his success from that point depended on his determination and his will to achieve.

The night prior to his transfer to the physical therapy unit I visited with Ray for the last time. I wondered for weeks if Ray would break down and begin to deal with the anger I felt sure he harbored. I wondered, but I decided not to ask.

Ray was watching the evening news as I entered the room. The story was breaking about a city struck by disaster, buildings leveled by an earthquake, homes destroyed, lives lost.

"Have a seat, Doc," he said. "I was just watching this story about the earthquake. Terrible, isn't it? All those poor people, homeless, jobless. I really feel for them."

I was amazed. How could Ray possibly think about anyone else after what had happened to him? But he was concerned for the people. Even after what he had been through, Ray had compassion for his fellow human beings in pain.

I could stand it no longer. I had to know more. Before I realized it, I was in the midst of asking Ray the question I had wanted to ask for some time: "Ray, aren't you upset about what happened to you? Haven't you been overcome with anger and resentment? Haven't you felt the injustice of it all? Haven't you felt, you know, a little bitter?"

He looked at me and smiled. "Yeah, Doc, I guess I did feel a little bitter at first. I wondered why this accident occurred. I especially wondered, *Why me?* But then I thought about it, and I thought, *Why* not *me?* Why would I think that I was so special that nothing bad could ever happen to me? I know God still takes care of me. I know He still loves me, and as long as I've got that, I think I can deal with just about anything. There is a lot of strength in knowing something like that."

Sometimes the most important lessons are taught to a classroom of one, and for me, school was in session. I was absolutely stunned by what he said. Ray had single-handedly managed to take all of the fun out of the little pity party I had been having for myself that week. I was simultaneously overcome with the emotions of admiration and humiliation. I shook Ray's hand, told him how much I had enjoyed being involved in his care, and left the room a better person for having known him.

It happened again, just the other day. It was the end of another busy afternoon, charts were signed, phone calls were made, dictations were all finished. I was about to leave the office when the beeper sounded. I winced momentarily. After all, it had been a difficult day, and it was supposed to be over. I'm not sure why, maybe it was the fact that the beep came exactly at five o'clock, but for some reason I found myself thinking about Ray. I wondered how he was doing and what the rest of his rehab had been like. I wondered if he was still experiencing a lot of pain. I wondered if he was learning to walk again, if he was learning to deal with his disability. I looked down at my feet as they carried me effortlessly to the phone and realized that my day had not been all that difficult. In fact, I knew my life in general was not really so hard. I remembered what Ray had told me about the Source of his strength, and suddenly, I felt that I, too, could deal with just about anything.

Chapter 3

THE MAN BEHIND
THE GLASSES

Antonio was really a likable young man with an infectious personality. But he wasn't exactly the kind of person you would want hanging around with your kids. Antonio had grown up quickly, a hard-nosed product of the tough inner city. He had been introduced to the realities of life, and to the gang system, at a very young age. By the time he was ten, he began hanging around the wrong kind of people, and by age fourteen, he was the wrong kind of person.

His spin on the story was a little different. He viewed himself as "a victim of a few misunderstandings." He said he was just "a struggling small businessman" trying to get by. On more than one occasion, however, his business had been shut down. Antonio had twice been arrested for the sale of illegal substances, and at least once he was admitted to a rehab unit for powdering his nose (on the inside).

When I saw him that night, he had been in "somewhat of a dispute." Those were his words, mind you. From the description of the events it sounded more like a street brawl to me. I realized, as I listened, just what a rough-looking character Antonio was. He had a bright red bandanna stylishly wrapped around his head, jet-black leather jacket and matching boots, and the facial expression of someone who had gone looking for trouble and found it.

According to his version of the story, Antonio had been confronted by "two dudes" who had "jumped him," and Antonio had pulled a knife. Antonio had broken two rules. The first one was a law, the one about carrying a concealed weapon. The second was a commonsense rule, the one about not pulling a knife at a gunfight. Just for the record, as surely as scissors beats paper, gun *will* beat knife every time.

"Kinda tough luck, huh, Antonio? Running into a couple of guys with a gun."

"Yeah, Doc, I guess it was. The only reason I ever carried that knife in the first place was to defend myself."

"So you would never have used it unless it was absolutely necessary, right?" I asked him.

"Doc, you know that's true. But if I felt like I had to, I woulda cut those dudes the three ways you want to be cut the least—long, deep, and very frequently."

I pondered his deep philosophical statement as I turned my attention back to his wounds. I knew that Antonio wouldn't have come to the E.R. unless he truly feared for his life. I guess the blood scared him. He was covered in it, and it was all his own.

We started an IV line on Antonio, cross-matched four units of blood, and sent a stat blood count to the lab as we took every precaution to stabilize him. He may have appeared to be in no danger, but it was a gunshot wound and nothing to be taken lightly. I carefully removed the pressure dressing to get a better look at the area and discovered a large damaged artery. The spray of blood three feet into the air convinced me it was a dressing better left in place, so I held pressure and waited for the arrival of the vascular surgeon. The wound was a small one, just above the knee, but clearly, the arterial damage needed to be repaired.

Even with all the excitement, the blood, the leather, and the bandanna weren't the first things I noticed as I entered the room that night. Antonio was proudly sporting a nice pair of beachworthy sunglasses. This seemed odd since it was two o'clock in the morning, and the E.R. lights, though adequate, were not blinding. I assumed Antonio preferred that I not get any real close looks at his pupil size. Dilated pupils are often a sign of recent drug use. I couldn't help myself, though; I had to pursue it if only out of curiosity.

"Antonio," I said, "why the dark glasses? Do I need to turn the lights down a little?"

He laughed, cocked his head backward, and replied, "You know, Doc, when you bad, you bad twenty-four hours a day."

I couldn't help smiling. As I said, he really was a likable person.

While I stood there applying pressure to his leg wound, the thought occurred to me that perhaps I shouldn't have given him such a hard time about the shades. After all, that's just human nature, isn't it, to hide behind masks? I realized that I, too, in a manner of speaking had gained a measure of expertise in hiding behind my own dark glasses.

A particular incident came to mind. It happened one Sunday morning as I was driving my family to worship. I was all dressed up and sparkling clean, at least on the outside, in a nice suit, starched shirt, shined shoes, and a silk tie. We came to a traffic light, and there *he* was. I tried to run through the light, but I couldn't, so we stopped right by him. You've seen the guy I'm talking about, the haggard-looking guy in ragged clothes and worn-out shoes. And there *it* was, the cardboard sign: WILL WORK FOR FOOD. Boy, he was pulling out all the stops. He had worked the guilt thing to perfection!

It's not that I didn't want to help him, you understand, but I was on my way to church for goodness' sake. What did you expect me to do? Be late? I just stared ahead and pretended not to notice him.

I knew exactly what I had to do. My challenge was to avoid eye contact with the guy. *I'll bet he's a con man*, I thought. *Yeah, that's it. He's a con man. Probably has a pocket full of money from a bunch of suckers not nearly as smart as I am.* That thought eased my conscience, at least momentarily.

My children, however, were not quite so astute. I turned toward the backseat and was horrified to see their eyes glued on the man. I feared it would be years before they could perfect my technique of looking the other way. My horror was compounded when my five-year-old daughter, Lindsay, spoke up and asked, "Dad, why is that man standing there?"

For heaven's sake, will this light never change? Finally, I drove away as I began to explain, "Honey, that man is there asking for money, but he might already have some, and he might not really be poor, and he might use it for beer, and besides, don't ask so many questions."

I looked to my wife, Deb, for support, but she gave none. I glanced back over my shoulder, hoping my weak explanation had deterred my daughter, but it hadn't. Then came the final blow. With tears streaming down her face, Lindsay said, "But, Daddy, if he isn't poor, then why is he dressed like that?"

"Oh, well, you see, honey, I uh . . . that is, uh . . . help me out here, Deb."

There was a long pause as they all glared at me. "Okay," I said, "I'm turning the car around." We drove back to the intersection, and there he was, sign still in hand. I looked quickly into my wallet, hoping I could slip him a small bill and get on with my life.

"Hmm, two twenties," I mumbled.

"Deb, do you have a ten?"

That didn't go over well, either. Okay, so some of us are slower learners than others. I reluctantly handed him the twenty and prepared to drive away, glad that the ugly incident was over. But as I did, something stopped me. I happened to notice two small hands reaching from the backseat window. Lindsay and Christopher, my three-year-old son, were handing the man their dollar bills that had been destined for the collection plate at church. The man took the money, thanked them, and said, "God bless you," as he waved good-bye. I swallowed hard on the lump that was stuck in my throat.

I looked in my rearview mirror to see two smiling, happy faces. They were the innocent faces of two children who had not yet learned to be judgmental, children who made a generous gift from the heart to some scruffy-looking stranger whose name they didn't even know.

But I saw something else as I gazed in that mirror, something I didn't like very much. Me. I saw someone who needed to change his view of things, someone who needed an attitude adjustment, someone who needed to look at life through a new pair of glasses.

I saw the same man on the street corner the other day, same clothes, same shoes, same sign. I don't know if he is a con man or not. It doesn't really matter. But I do know one thing. As I look at him through my new glasses, he doesn't look repulsive at all. In fact, he looks amazingly similar to me.

Chapter 4

THE SEA OF WORRY

Jake had been a farmer for more than forty-five years, and by all indications, he was very good at it. The people who knew him said his fields were always perfectly maintained, his equipment spotless, and his crops tremendous. Even at a time when other farmers seemed to be suffering financial difficulties, Jake continued to prosper. He had never borrowed any money as far as anyone knew. All his accounts were up to date. He dealt only in cash. Some seemed to wonder how he was able to do it, but those who knew him knew his secret. It was really no secret. It was just hard work. He was in his fields from sunrise till after dark, digging, planting, sweating, making sure everything was as it should be. No, Jake's success was no mistake. It was the fruit of his labor. He had earned it.

But people who knew Jake well also knew something else about him. They knew he was a chronic worrier. He worried about the weather, insects, weeds, and anything else that he perceived as a potential threat to his crops. But still his biggest worry, the one that would be his undoing, was his constant anxiety over his finances. Jake had survived the depression, and in his younger years he had known some pretty rough times. He had lived in a few makeshift houses and, as a child, had missed more than his share of meals. Jake had experienced firsthand the hardship of one serious financial crisis, and he was determined to avoid another at all costs.

Friends said they had noticed that over the last few years, his concerns over money had increased. He had become suspicious of almost everyone, convinced that those he had dealt with in the past were intent on taking advantage of him. He became more and more withdrawn. Rarely was he seen in town, and when he was seen, it was related only to business. He appeared angry, even suspicious, they would later say. He didn't seem to enjoy anyone's company anymore. Jake liquidated all his funds and kept them at home. He seemed to think it was safer that way.

In retrospect, it would be easy to say that Jake was severely depressed, even borderline psychotic.

At the time, however, his actions seemed appropriate, if eccentric. Everyone thought that was part of his personality as a chronic worrier.

Most of what I know about Jake, I learned from his friends and family. I was trying to piece his story together on a day filled with sadness and confusion. According to family members, Jake had become increasingly distant during the last week. He was especially preoccupied with his money. At the age of seventy-one, still working full time, Jake was concerned about not being able to retire. He worried about how he would survive, where he would live, who would take care of him. It had become an obsession.

Early that week he had seen his physician, complaining of stomach cramps. Workup at that time had been negative, and Jake was given an antispasmodic medication as well as a few sedatives to help him calm down.

That very same night he visited the local E.R., complaining of the same cramps. The evaluation was again unremarkable, and Jake was sent home in good condition with the same advice. Take your medication and relax!

Later, the true purpose of the visits would be known. They were desperate cries for help. They were the last gasps for air heard from a drowning man. A very wealthy, very frightened, and very anxious man was drowning in his self-created sea of worry.

Two days later Jake would make his final visit to his physician. In addition to the abdominal cramps, he complained of back pain. Again, a thorough evaluation was done. X rays were taken, blood samples and a urinalysis were evaluated, but nothing amiss could be found. Physically, Jake was the picture of health. Emotionally, he was suffering. His physician, now frustrated himself, spoke frankly with Jake that day. He prescribed an antidepressant and told him to slow down and take some time off, but Jake would have none of it.

Shortly after that, Jake began to put his plan into effect. He returned home that evening, ate dinner, then sat down and started to get his affairs in order. He carefully cataloged deeds, insurance policies, and all of his important papers. Before Jake retired that night, he made sure that every document of any importance regarding his life was in plain view on his kitchen table. He wanted to be sure his finances were taken care of appropriately. Even though his estate was in order, Jake was overcome with the fear that he might possibly outlive his ability to support himself. It was a thought he decided he couldn't tolerate: the idea of struggling financially, being forced to move from his home, maybe even going hungry. He had been there before, and he wasn't going back. Jake had convinced himself that there was only one way out, and he was determined to take it. He spelled it out for all to see in the note.

Early the next morning a jogger made his way past Jake's place. The man paused, ran in place for a moment, then waved and said good morning to Jake, just as he had always done. But there was no response. "He seemed a little preoccupied," the man later said.

"Jake was just standing there, cleaning his shotgun. Nothing seemed out of the ordinary." Nothing, that is, until he jogged to the end of the street and heard the blast behind him. The man turned, ran back up the street, and saw Jake lying there in a pool of his own blood.

The rescue crew was there within minutes, but their efforts were of little use. As they rolled Jake into the E.R., one of the nurses commented to me, "He was just in here a couple of days ago. I thought he'd be doing better by now." But it was clear he hadn't been doing better. It was truly an awful sight. Jake had put the barrel of the shotgun directly against his throat.

I quickly put on gloves and tried to see past the blood. I could visualize nothing. I knew I had to establish an airway if there was any chance of saving him, so I inserted my hand into the wound, hoping to feel something that would help me. Instead, I felt something sharp. I tried to look calm, but I knew I was feeling the remains of his cervical spine. I knew nothing else could be done, so I stopped the code. It was finished. Jake was dead.

I learned from his family that in addition to his papers, more than thirty thousand dollars in cash was found in Jake's house. *How sad,* I thought, *that Jake would be so obsessed with what lay ahead, even to the point of suicide.* Especially sad, in light of the fact that he had the resources to live well. But what he lacked—peace of mind—was much more valuable.

I stood in the conference room that day and talked with the family members at length, trying to help them through a difficult time. I remember the comments of one of Jake's sons in particular. He wiped his eyes and told me, "I think what Dad really needed was the assurance from someone that things were going to be okay. I think if he'd had that, if he'd really been able to believe it, I know he'd still be with us today." He then looked away and whispered, "But I guess we all need that, don't we?"

I patted him on the back, told him to let me know if there was any way I could help, and left the room thinking about his statements. And you know, I guess what he said was right. If we had a promise of that magnitude, we would have no more cause for worry, would we? If we just had some kind of guarantee, someone to assure us that ultimately, everything would be okay, life would be so much easier for all of us.

As I drove home that evening, I couldn't seem to forget the conversation I'd had with Jake's son. I wondered if I, too, had fallen victim to the trap that had claimed the life of his father. I wondered if the weight and worry of the world had occasionally gotten to me as well. I opened my Bible that night and by chance turned to the words of Jesus as He talked to His disciples in Matthew 6. It was interesting to listen to Him warn them against worry. I absorbed His words as He told them to give no thought to what they would eat, where they would live, or what they would wear. I felt slightly embarrassed as He reminded them that even the fowls of the air and flowers of the field are cared for by a loving God. Suddenly, I enjoyed a deep sense of comfort that I had not felt before. It was as if a gentle hand was patting me on the shoulder and telling me to claim the promise that was given by our Lord. Finally I remembered why this was so important, why we shouldn't be bothered with the cares of this world. I remembered that God does assure us that, ultimately, everything *will* be okay.

Chapter 5

CALL ME THOMAS

From the first day of fall practice it was obvious that the kid was going to be very special. Something about his presence on the court—maybe it was his determination—let the coaching staff know that he was in a class by himself. A few times last season he had shown great promise, but nothing like this. He was definitely going places. He had spent many long, grueling hours in training during the summer, lifting weights, running stairs, shooting free throws, and his efforts were beginning to pay off.

His family hoped the big payoff was still to come. They firmly believed he had the natural ability to play basketball in the NBA. Of course, there are no guarantees in life, yet the kid appeared to be a "can't miss" prospect if one ever existed. If he would continue to work and improve, if he would excel during his senior year in high school, then his dreams could become a reality.

Such were the hopes of a young basketball star named Thomas. Few people knew him by that name. Most called him Duke, after his favorite college team, the team he wanted to play for more than anything else on earth.

I had seen clips of Duke on the evening news, and he was an impressive athlete. He literally appeared to be a man playing among children. His size, quickness, and agility were far superior to those of his competition, and as a result he created havoc for opposing teams. Basketball scouts rated him as one of the top forwards in the entire South, and his name appeared on the short list of hopeful recruits for some of the best programs in the country.

None of that, however, mattered today. The only matter of importance was the game, and it was a big one: the state semifinals. The game plan, as usual, had been developed around Duke, and as usual, he had delivered. Great players usually do during big games. But with time running out, and with the outcome of the game still very much in doubt, Duke knew it was time to raise his level of performance. It was time to add another chapter to the remarkable tale of the local hoops legend.

The final minutes of the game were very exciting. Duke turned in several more big plays, but the demands placed on him were beginning to take their toll. He began to tire. Moments later, following a steal, Duke raced down the court for a break-away dunk, but the trailing defender had other ideas. The frustration of watching Duke dominate the game had become too much for him, so he undercut Duke's legs, sending his body flying several feet into the air. Duke fell awkwardly to the floor, sustaining a sharp, painful blow to the base of his neck. He slowly pulled himself to his feet as he noticed a tingling sensation over his entire body. He stumbled to the sideline, and a time-out was quickly called while the coaches and trainers frantically worked to return Duke to the action. But Duke wasn't quite sure.

"Something's not right, Coach. My neck is hurting. I think I might have been paralyzed for a second out there. I'm not sure I can go back in."

The coach, caught up in the excitement of the moment, would have none of that. "Don't think you can go back in!" he barked. "Son, the game . . . the whole season is on the line. Y-y-y-you don't have a choice! You *have* to go back in!"

With those words, Duke was momentarily embarrassed by his lapse of courage. He knew his coach was counting on him; his team was depending on him; his family was banking on him. He knew he couldn't let them all down. With his strength beginning to return, he tossed his towel at the trainer's feet and raced back onto the court, much to the approval of the roaring crowd. The team lined up for the inbounds play and waited for the whistle. It was obviously not the time for any trick plays. It was Duke's moment. There was no doubt about it. The tension in the gym was almost palpable.

As the inbounds pass was made to Duke, you could almost feel the contact from the sidelines, the bodies banging against each other, elbows flying wildly. But as the ball was just clearing the net, it became obvious that something was very wrong. Duke had taken another hard blow to the neck and was lying facedown and motionless on the court. The shot was good. He had made the turnaround jumper, but it would be his last. Duke could not get up.

The silence of the crowd was ominous as the trainers rushed to his aid. Duke was not yet aware of it, but the course of his life had been irreversibly altered with the events of that one play. The fortunes of an athlete can quickly change, injuries can occur, and fragile dreams can easily be broken. Such was the case for the gifted young man.

With no limb movement and no feeling at all below midchest, Duke was taken from the court on a protective stretcher and transported to our emergency department. Rolling through the E.R. doors, he seemed so out of place in his full uniform, his knee pads, his large leather sneakers. He was visibly shaken and nervous, but he tried his best to cooperate with my instructions.

"I'm doing the best I can, Doc," he told me. "I just can't move anything."

I chatted with him while I examined his extremities, trying to put him at ease. Next I explained the nature of the MRI scan we would be doing and why we needed to get a closer look at his neck.

The scan revealed a large fracture in his cervical spine as well as severe swelling and significant disruption of the spinal cord. My heart sank when the radiologist reviewed the films with me. As I was returning to the E.R. with the films, I saw several other team members in the hallway. I made eye contact with several and noticed they all shared the same blank facial expression. There was an eerie absence of conversation in the group—no small talk, no discussion of the outcome of the game. It was almost as if it had never taken place, and in truth, it hardly seemed important now.

Duke was immediately taken to surgery and treated with the latest in medication and modern technology, but over the next few days, we knew with certainty that his basketball career was over. My only hope was that he would someday be able to walk again. After the surgery, I had the opportunity to talk with him in more detail, and his details of the events of the game revealed what had happened. Duke had almost certainly fractured his neck on the initial fall, causing the numbness, tingling, and muscle weakness. That injury, though unstable, could potentially have been corrected and further damage prevented if only he hadn't returned to the game. The second injury was the one that caused the paralysis.

Despite aggressive physical therapy and all the medication he was given, Duke never regained any of his motor functions. He left the hospital several weeks later in a wheelchair. On the night prior to his discharge I spoke with him one last time and asked him about his plans for the future. I heard the voice of a person suffering from intense pain, more pain than could be attributed to his physical injury alone. He had been stripped of his very identity. There would be no more field goals for him, yet there were still goals. He told me he wanted to go to college, to get a job, to make something of his life. He told me he knew he would miss basketball, but he still hoped to make his family proud of him. He told me he was worried about his mother and asked me to see how she was holding up. Just before I left the room, Duke had one final request for me.

"Can I ask you to do one more thing for me, Doc?"

"Sure you can. You just name it."

"If you don't mind, would you just call me Thomas from now on?"

My heart sank once again as I assured him I didn't mind at all.

I looked around the room at the cards, letters, and flowers from caring friends and adoring fans. Hanging above his head was a GET WELL sign from the cheering squad. A picture of his girlfriend sat by the phone. His letterman's jacket was neatly folded and draped across the foot of the bed. On his nightstand were letters from several prominent college coaches, letters of encouragement, but I knew they would someday stop arriving. I knew Thomas's name would most likely be lost in the shuffle. Although I'm sure the concern of the recruiters was genuine, I knew Thomas's name was on a list that would be replaced with one containing the next class of prospects.

I was greatly saddened as I thought how terrible it was, not that a career in basketball had been lost, but that Thomas had been sentenced to life with a disability because of a few brief words of bad advice. I wondered how many times that had happened in my life. How many times I heard that voice telling me what I had to do . . . what I needed to try . . . what was expected of me. I realized at that moment that advice can be a powerful tool, and it can also be a dangerous weapon.

Thomas now knew that as well. He knew he had turned to one he had trusted to guide him through a difficult decision. He had literally placed his life in the hands of another, yet he could not have known that the counsel he had received had someone else's best interest at heart. They were valuable lessons he had learned, but unfortunately, there was nothing that could be done to reverse the tragedy. They were lessons he learned too late.

Chapter 6

PORTRAIT OF A HEALTHY HEART

"My chest still hurts" were the first words out of John's mouth that morning. That wasn't exactly what I wanted to hear. You see, when I asked John how he was feeling, I intended it to be a rhetorical question, just part of my normal routine. Funny, though, how people with heart disease seem to skip over all the idle chitchat and cut right to the chase.

John was not in the mood for engaging in small talk. He had no use for trivial expenditures of his time. But there was something else I noticed about John. His smile was gone. Usually, John was a very happy person, very outgoing, but not that day. We were there to talk serious business. Smiles were not in order.

John was a very distinguished-looking gentleman. His suits appeared to be tailored, his shoes were always perfectly polished, and his jet-black hair was always neatly in place. I'm sure he could strike quite an impressive pose in the boardroom, but he appeared slightly less imposing as I looked at him. John was in my office to discuss the results of his recent treadmill test, and the report was not good. He hadn't performed as well as he had expected; he was able to walk only a few minutes before being overcome by fatigue. The worst part for him was that he knew he had done his best.

"There was some concern over some electrical changes on the monitor," he said, though he didn't understand exactly what the cardiologist had meant by the statement. He remembered distinctly the presence of some "reversible perfusion abnormalities" that were present on his radiological scans. Sound serious? It is. John knew all too well what that part meant.

"Blockage, right, Doc?"

"I'm afraid so," I answered.

John closed his eyes and hung his head after hearing my reply. He knew what was to come next. John had heard the diagnosis before, twice to be exact. The scenario was becoming all too familiar to him. He knew a return visit to the cardiologist would soon follow, and an appointment would need to be scheduled for yet another arteriogram. He knew there would be painful needles, tubes, X rays, more needles, and endless personal questions. After all that unbridled fun and excitement, he would most likely be called on to endure another bypass operation. As you might have guessed, that wasn't exactly what John wanted to hear, either. He wasn't sure he wanted to go through all that again. To be honest, I'm not sure he believed he was up to the task, but he knew something had to be done. If he knew anything for sure, he knew he couldn't continue living as he had been the last few months.

John had always been the athletic type, but recently, he had been forced to give up most of his activities, even his weekly golf game. He was too embarrassed to admit to his friends that he didn't have the stamina to finish the full eighteen holes. He also enjoyed swimming laps in his pool, but he just didn't have the energy anymore. Simple yard work and minor household chores had become major undertakings for him. It was not much of an existence for a once active sixty-year-old man, but I was trying to help John make the best of it. He looked for a few moments as if he were considering throwing in the towel, but I knew he wouldn't. Not John.

We had a long talk about his family. We talked about the possibility of his applying for disability payments to help him cut down on work and reduce his stress level. We also talked about how ironic it is that it takes something like a serious health condition to make you realize what's really important in life and put things in proper perspective. That's when he said it, and it took me a little by surprise.

With a tear forming in the corner of his eye, John looked at me and said, "You know, Doc, I've finally realized, when your heart's not right, there's not much else that really matters."

I didn't know how to respond, other than to nod in agreement. I knew he was right. I also knew he had been struggling with a question that can't be answered in any of our high-tech angiography suites. Although John may have been specifically referring to his physical blood-pumping organ, the ramifications of his statement penetrate much deeper than that. I could tell John was dealing with some very important issues of the heart.

It must have been an especially difficult problem in John's mind. After all, by everyone's standards he had succeeded in life. He had built a large company from the ground up. He had bought and sold, hired and fired, and conquered the corporate monster in the process. Yet something in his life seemed to be lacking. Something wasn't quite right, but he couldn't tell exactly what it was yet. He would need a little more time to figure that out.

I arrived at the office one day last week and was pleasantly surprised to see John's name on my schedule for the afternoon. He was coming in for a routine postoperative visit, and he looked absolutely great, especially in his new casual attire. He had traded in the expensive tailored clothes for a nylon jogging suit, a T-shirt, and a pair of tennis shoes. He sat down, pulled off his shoes, and raised the pants leg to display his new scars. They were healing nicely. His chest was also doing quite well. And it seemed his walk was a little slower than usual, as expected.

However, what was most noticeable that day was John's smile. It was most definitely back. I couldn't help wondering to myself, *What made the difference? Why the smile?* We had much the same talk as we had had on his last visit. We talked again about his family. We filled out some preliminary papers, applying for disability payments with his insurance company. We even talked about how John had used the surgery as an opportunity to concentrate more fully on what was really important in life. But there were no tears in his eyes. All I saw was the anticipation of enjoyment from a man determined to make the most of whatever time he has left.

"Yeah, Doc, I did some thinking after I left your office the last time. I know I seemed pretty upset, but it wasn't really about the surgery. I was more concerned that I might leave my wife and kids and I didn't know them as well as I should. To tell you the truth, my business has demanded so much of me over the last few years, I haven't had time to do much of anything with my family. But that's all changed now. I'm going to make sure they understand just how much I care for them. Believe me, I'm going to see to that."

I scheduled a time for his return in another four weeks, and I told him I was very pleased with the progress he had made thus far. As he left the office that day, I looked at John in a completely different light. I no longer saw an aggressive businessman. I saw a man who knew what was really important to him. A man who was determined to be the best father, the best husband, he could be. A man who, despite the pain, despite the scars and grafts, was leading a more enjoyable life, one of the many benefits of living with a healthy heart.

John's experience has been helpful to me as well because it made me determine to keep a closer watch on the state of affairs in my heart. After all, what John said makes an awful lot of sense. When your heart's not right, there's not much else that really matters.

Chapter 7

SECOND CHANCES

I could hardly believe what I was seeing. I was fast beginning to think that maybe, just maybe, Jimmy was not very bright. I tried to give him the benefit of the doubt, but the truth was, he seemed intent on *proving* that he was not very bright. The evidence was beginning to look a bit overwhelming. He was standing before me with wet hair, wet clothes, wet shoes, and a mangled metallic contraption wrapped around his head. It was the culmination of a very strange story that had begun a couple of weeks earlier.

Jimmy was the prototypical college fraternity member. His blood was blue, his credit cards gold, and his sports car imported. It was only the best for young Jimmy. On the weekends, his activities centered around partying with his fraternity buddies and basically having a good time. That was how his problem began.

One weekend, Jimmy and some of his friends

decided to go on a boating trip to a nearby lake, and, as usual, they took their favorite cold brewed liquid refreshment along with them. After skiing for a while, and after giving their beverage selection adequate time to impair both their mental and their physical skills, they decided it might be interesting to expand their horizons and try something new. Wouldn't it be more fun to try something really exciting, such as performing some jumps from a ramp they could quickly construct on Jimmy's pier?

Their discussion concluded that it would indeed be the perfect ending to the outing. Before long, with the ingenious use of some old plywood, their makeshift ramp was in place. After adequately testing it for safety, the first of the group tried his jump, then another and another.

"Not too bad," they shouted from the water. The jumps hadn't been anything spectacular, but there were no major injuries, just some big splashes.

It was now Jimmy's turn, but as Jimmy prepared for his run, he knew he wouldn't be satisfied with the mediocre. He looked down at his friends and tried to decide what it would take for him to adequately showcase his unique skills. Then it hit him. He would stretch the limits by diving instead of jumping.

The run started innocently enough, just like all

the others. As he was approaching the ramp, he judged the sun and accounted for the wind. Then he did it; he executed an almost perfect flip and hit the water with all the grace and beauty of a two-hundred-pound safe. At the moment of impact his neck snapped backward, and Jimmy was unable to move. "I'm paralyzed," were the first words from his mouth as he rose to the surface of the lake.

His friends quickly rescued him from the water, saving his life, and called for medical assistance. Jimmy came into the E.R. by ambulance with a stiff foam collar supporting his neck, protecting his precious spinal cord. By then, the feeling had returned to Jimmy's arms and legs. He could move his fingers and wiggle his toes. His muscle strength was good throughout all extremities, and his reflexes revealed no abnormality.

Amazingly enough, no neurological deficit was noted, but Jimmy was not out of the woods yet. An MRI revealed a small fracture at the base of his skull, but more important a fractured vertebra in his cervical spine. It was a dangerous and unstable fracture. It was the proverbial broken neck your mom always warned you'd get if you did something you shouldn't. It was clearly a very delicate situation. The neck, in its compromised condition, was vulnerable to any repeat trauma. Any further movement, any slight blow to the neck, might result in permanent damage, possibly total paralysis. The fracture would have to be repaired immediately.

Within a matter of hours an experienced neuro-surgeon performed the operation to repair the injured area. It was a lengthy procedure and a very difficult one, but the surgery was successful. Jimmy escaped the incident without paralysis. He was very lucky and very thankful.

Due to his youth and overall good health, Jimmy recovered quickly. He mastered his physical therapy and left the hospital a week later wearing a halo, a large round metal object secured to his head during the surgery. It was placed in an attempt to protect him from suffering any further damage to his spine. Strict instructions were given regarding his activity and follow-up. He was told he would have specific limitations regarding any physical exertion. He was also reminded that he would need close monitoring as an outpatient since he would be required to wear the halo for some time.

After his discharge, Jimmy's friends came to visit and decided to take him out to celebrate his recovery. It was the least they could do since they had survived such an ordeal together. Before long, they were back at the same lake, drinking the same beverages, developing the same mental and physical impairments. They began discussing how the accident had happened in the first place, and before long there was some talk about reconstructing the ramp.

A couple of the guys even mentioned a desire to try the jump again, and eventually, one did, then another and another. But Jimmy just sat in the boat, looking over the site of his near fatal accident, wondering what he had done wrong. He knew he had kept a tight tucked position during his descent. That couldn't have been his mistake. Maybe it was the elements. This time there was no sun in his eyes, no wind.

If I had it to do over again, I'd concentrate more on my landing, he thought to himself. He knew he could pull it off if he could try again, so he did. I know. It was hard for me to believe, too, but he really did. Once again he performed an almost perfect flip, halo and all, and once again, he hit the water like a two-hundred-pound safe.

Jimmy made another trip to the E.R. that afternoon, and he stood before me as I described earlier, wet hair, wet clothes, wet shoes, and a mangled metallic halo wrapped around his head. Other than a terrible headache, he was none the worse for wear. I performed a thorough neurological exam and ordered more films of his neck, all of which were normal. At this juncture, I couldn't decide whether to pity his ignorance or admire his indestructibility, so I did both. I also spent several minutes on the phone trying to convince his neurosurgeon that I wasn't kidding him, that Jimmy was in the E.R. and needed a few minor adjustments to his halo.

After the smoke cleared, I had the opportunity to talk to Jimmy in more depth. He told me he would be graduating soon. "I hope to get into medical school," he told me.

"Well, you know you'll have to survive college first," I replied. We both laughed for a moment after that. Finally, though, I had to ask him, "What were you thinking? What could possibly have been going through your mind at the moment you decided to put on those skis and try your jump again?" All he could say was he thought he had figured out where he went wrong. It was his takeoff. He wasn't pushing off the ramp with enough force to start the jump. Pushing off harder would allow him to rotate his body forward and greatly improve his landing. I felt sure he would work on that next time.

As he was leaving the E.R., Jimmy's surgeon asked me, "What does it take to get through to some people? How many times can a person make the same stupid mistake and get away with it?" I had no answer, but I knew if such records were kept, Jimmy would be a serious challenger for the title.

I also knew that Jimmy was a very fortunate young man. Fortunate that the human body was designed with amazing resilience. Fortunate that his friends and the neurosurgeon were able to get to him in time. Fortunate that ours is a world where second, sometimes even third, chances are granted.

I never knew if Jimmy tried his jump again. I wonder, though, and I think the odds are pretty good that he did. Nevertheless, I was glad Jimmy was okay, glad he survived his accidents, glad he was granted a couple of extra chances in life. And even though I had to admit that Jimmy probably wasn't the smartest guy I had ever known, something about him touched my heart. Something that reminded me that if I ever hope to have a halo of my own, I'm going to need a few second chances.

Chapter 8

THE HEALING HEM

Dale happens to be a very good friend, and contrary to popular belief, he is an extremely bright person, for an attorney, that is. That's why it was so hard to believe that he would do something like that to his own body, but that's his personality. He is a very independent, do-it-yourself kind of guy. That personality trait, by the way, did not develop by chance. There is a very good explanation for it.

Dale grew up in a good Christian home with loving parents. They disciplined him, loved him, and taught him to love God. When Dale was seven years old, however, his life was painfully disrupted. It was then that his father died of leukemia. He had developed the illness as a result of chemical weapons exposure while serving in the military. Little was known about the dangers of such exposure at that time, and even less was known about treating its related diseases. His physicians did all they could to save him, but despite their valiant efforts, he didn't respond to treatment. The family watched him quickly slip away. It was a terrible experience for Dale.

Times were tough after that, and though they struggled financially and emotionally, they managed to survive. His mother went to nursing school and got a job to support the family. Dale also worked very hard, determined to succeed in the classroom. It became an outlet for him to help him deal with the loss of his father.

When he got to college, his hard work and dedication continued. He began to solidify his career plans to fulfill his dream of becoming an attorney. By his senior year, his academic record was well established. He was within a year of finishing his undergraduate degree, and law school was close to becoming a reality. I tried my best to get him to attend medical school with me, but my attempts fell on deaf ears. Still, I knew that whatever he chose to do, he would be successful.

During the midst of our last year of college, tragedy struck Dale for the second time. This time was even worse because he felt a duty to take care of his mother, to shelter her and watch over her just as she had done for him all those years. That's why it was so hard to accept the fact that she had brain cancer and, worst of all, that her condition was incurable. Her physicians could do little but offer support. Again, Dale was forced to watch a parent die a painful death.

It was understandable, then, why Dale didn't quickly seek medical attention for most of his ailments. He hadn't exactly been inspired with an overwhelming degree of confidence in the field of medical science. His only significant exposure to doctors was listening to them explain why his parents weren't responding to any of their treatments and eventually why they couldn't be saved. And a hospital, well, that was the place you went just before you died. Dale figured he could do just about as well by himself. That's how he got into trouble.

About a week before he called me, Dale had developed a nagging case of athlete's foot. He tried everything that was available over the counter, the smelly powders, the sticky sprays, the oily lotions, but found no relief. That's when it occurred to him. He remembered that his mother, the nurse, had once treated him for a case of athlete's foot by applying a diluted solution of chlorine bleach directly to the rash. The wheels in his mind were turning at a feverish pace. But he also remembered his prior infection had been rather mild, not nearly as aggravating as his current condition, which would require more drastic measures. Dale reasoned, with the skill of any great barrister, that if diluted bleach was good, concentrated bleach would be even better. So he bought a large, economy-size bleach bottle (which, oddly enough, was not located with the other foot care products) and went home to effect his own cure. He poured the bleach into a large pan, settled into his easy chair, and confidently inserted his foot. The pain and swelling began almost immediately.

Several days later, when the pain was absolutely unbearable, he called and asked for advice. He pled his case brilliantly as he tried to convince me that his reasoning had indeed been sound, but I overruled him.

I instructed him to meet me in the E.R. so I could assess the damage, and it was substantial. The foot was swollen to nearly twice its normal size, and the skin was cracked and bleeding. I was now faced with a severe ethical dilemma. Would I take action to save the life of a lawyer? I struggled with my decision briefly and then elected to proceed. Broad-spectrum antibiotics were started immediately, and great care was taken to debride the foot of the dead and dying tissue. Several days of hospitalization followed, marked by numerous whirlpool treatments and further debridement. Dale was soon to realize he was very fortunate. He responded nicely to therapy, and the foot was saved. He would have no long-term damage. Dale and I reached an understanding the day I discharged him. I agreed I would not attempt to practice law, and he agreed he would make no further attempts to practice medicine. Thus far, it seems to be working well for both of us.

The adventure of Dale's foot infection is one we now recall with amusement, though at the time it was quite serious. His underlying problem, however, his lack of confidence in physicians, is not a new phenomenon. I remember reading another such story, one about a very ill woman, as told in the writings of another physician. The story occurred many years ago in a time when medicine was not nearly as advanced as it is today. The woman, I learned, had spent all her money on doctors, but no cure for her illness could be found. She had a condition that today would be classified as abnormal uterine bleeding, a condition totally curable by hysterectomy. In her time, however, people looked at her in disgust and proceeded to avoid her. For more than twelve years she had faced isolation, and no relief was in sight.

The physician wrote that "no doctor could heal her," but as I read his words I could sense there was more. He wrote with a tone I fully understood. He spoke as a physician, with anger toward incurable disease.

But the desperate woman's options were not totally exhausted. She had heard from friends of

One who might help, a specialist experienced in treating even the most dreadful disorders. She decided to make her way to His clinic but soon found that she had greatly underestimated His popularity. Without any money, and without an appointment, she feared she might never know His healing touch. Still she had come so far, and with no other options she decided to stay for a while. She stood there outside His office and waited for that one perfect moment to approach Him and tell Him of her condition. Maybe He would have mercy. Maybe some lifesaving medication would be dispensed, yet it was simply not to be. Even as He made His way home He was swarmed by crowds. She thought if she could just get close, surely He would see, surely He would help. But she never could seem to get close enough, so she just reached out and touched the hem of His coat. That's when it happened, and she knew it immediately. Everything they had told her about Him was true. She had been cured!

The once suffering soul, who thought she might never again know peace, had indeed found it. The patient who had little use for healers, who wondered if she would ever be free from her burden, had finally found the hem of the Great Physician. Her life was changed, her trust restored, and at long last she knew the joy of being made whole.

Chapter 9

REVENGE IS A DISH THAT'S BEST UNSERVED

The call came from the E.R. to let me know that she was there and that she was too sick to go home. I wasn't at all surprised. Her health had been rapidly declining over the last year. First there was the new onset of atrial fibrillation that brought on the bouts with congestive heart failure. Then there were the kidney infections, serious ones, one right after the other. I wondered how much more her body could endure, but her will to live was strong. She was quite a fighter.

Her name was Mrs. Jessica, but her friends (and there were many) called her Jessie. She was a sweet, gentle woman whose life was complicated by her complex medical problems. She now found herself in the E.R., being admitted to the hospital for treatment of pneumonia.

I entered the exam room and saw the eyes of a once proud spirit, now faced with the uncertainty of aging and the cold indignity of illness. As I spoke with her, I closed the door, then took a blanket and covered her partially exposed body. I knew I could do nothing about the aging process, but the issue of her indignity was certainly reversible.

She bounced back from the pneumonia, but on the day she was to be discharged, Jessie slipped in the shower, fell, and broke her hip. She cried for more than an hour, mostly from the pain, but also from the compounding frustration of it all.

Following the hip fracture and subsequent surgery, she seemed well on the road to recovery. Jessie's improvement, however, was rapidly detoured when she developed blood clots in her legs. The condition required blood thinners, and that meant still more time in the hospital. I remember thinking that certainly nothing else could go wrong, yet I dared not say so. I knew Murphy's Law need not be challenged in Jessie's case.

Considering what Jessie had been through, I couldn't have blamed her for complaining about her problems, but she didn't. That just wasn't her way, she said.

"Besides, it wouldn't do any good anyway. Better

to concentrate my energy on trying to get well," she told me. It was a commendable theory from a very remarkable woman. But even with all the positive thinking, Jessie did not recover from the blood clots as quickly as she would have liked.

After several days of doing well, she suddenly began to deteriorate. Her attitude changed as well; she became depressed and withdrawn. She wouldn't talk when I visited her, she refused her medications, and she noticeably lost weight. I was specifically puzzled by the weight loss because her dishes were always empty when I saw them. I ordered calorie counts to document the exact amount of her intake, and all appeared to be in order. Nevertheless, she still appeared malnourished and continued to lose weight.

I began to look for an underlying malignancy, thinking that was the reason for the unexplained weight loss, but I found nothing. Eventually, the gastroenterologist suggested that we put a feeding tube in Jessie and replace her diet with nutritional liquids. I thought it was unnecessary, but he felt it was the only way we could know for sure that her nutrition was adequate. That afternoon we placed the tube, and the improvement was almost immediate. Her strength returned, she was again pleasant, and her weight began to normalize. That's when the trouble started.

The following day I received a phone message from her son, whom I didn't know existed until his call, threatening a lawsuit if we didn't start feeding his mother. I tried to reach him to explain our treatment plan, but I was unsuccessful. When I returned to visit Jessie that evening, there was another note on the chart: "Son is very upset about his mother's care. Says he will sue. Not happy with the physician."

The next day I was finally able to contact her son by phone. I assured him that his mother was being well fed through the nasogastric tube, and that he had no reason for concern. My explanation seemed to make him angrier. I tried to reason with him, but I couldn't get a word in edgewise.

"I want three meals a day sent to her room or else!" That was his parting threat as he slammed down the phone.

I was beginning to lose my patience. As I made rounds that evening, I debated whether or not to bring up the conversation to Jessie, but I decided I should. I sat on the corner of her bed and reluctantly told her the entire story of my interaction with her son. I was hoping she could shed some light on the confusing situation, but her reaction took me by surprise. When Jessie learned of her son's behavior, she was visibly shaken and extremely embarrassed.

"Doc, I'm ashamed to have to say this about any-one, especially my own son, but that boy ain't nothing but trouble. Truth is, he never has been."

She began to cry as she shared the story of her relationship with her abusive son. Jessie confessed that he had been stealing from her for years, taking her household money, selling off her personal items, cashing her Social Security checks, all to support his drug habit. He had been in and out of jail repeatedly, but he never seemed to stay very long at a time. For the first ten days of Jessie's hos-pitalization, he hadn't been able to find her. She was very happy because even though she was sick, she had a brief period of peace. It was something she hadn't experienced in a long time.

Finally, he found out where she was, and he had been coming to the hospital to "visit" her. Three times a day he would come, to terrorize her, to intimidate her, to eat her food. Then he would leave, but not before he threatened to kill her if she told anyone. Her pitiful story of abuse was (and is) all too real and all too common.

I was furious. Threatening me with a lawsuit was bad enough, but endangering the health of his own mother—well, it was more than I could stand. I alerted hospital security as well as the local police department. They watched diligently for him over the next several days, but he was nowhere to be found. I guess he was wise to us because he never showed his face again.

As much as I tried to be understanding, to realize that he had a very serious drug problem and needed help, I couldn't seem to let go of my anger. I couldn't imagine how low one would have to go before he would steal food from his sick mother. I must admit I wanted justice for Jessie and revenge for me. I was moved to the point of wanting to do serious bodily harm to that jerk, even though I knew that wasn't the right response.

I watched the situation closely during the next week, and I was amazed at Jessie's recovery. With the help of social workers we arranged a place for her in a safer environment where we hoped her son couldn't harm her anymore. I wondered, however, when he might surface again, with further intimidation for her and more threats for me. I was still very angry and absolutely unforgiving.

Even several weeks after Jessie's discharge, I found myself thinking about the horrible situation. For some reason I couldn't overcome my feelings that the young man was due a large dose of justice, and I desperately wanted to serve it! Thoughts of revenge kept playing in my mind.

My change of heart came a few days later when I saw Jessie in the office for follow-up. I knew things were going well for her because she looked better than she had in years. Still, I had to know if her life was really back in order, if she had had more trouble from him.

"Jessie, how's your son doing?" I casually asked.

"I haven't seen him," she said. "Don't know exactly where he is, and maybe that's for the best." But then came the surprise.

"You know, I sure do hope that boy gets himself straightened out someday," she told me. "I'd hate to think anything bad would happen to him. I know he's been a lot of trouble, Doc, but even so, he's still my son, and I'll always love him. Maybe if I could get him to see you, you could help me get him cleaned up."

It was a reply I had definitely not expected, and it caused me to be more than a little embarrassed about what I had been thinking. As I watched Jessie leave the office that day, I realized I had underestimated the love a parent can feel for even the most wayward of children. After all, no matter what he had done, he would always be her child. I realized at that moment that I owed the wonderful woman a debt of gratitude because she helped me learn a significant lesson. Thanks to her I now understand a little more about what it means to forgive and a lot more about what it means to be forgiven.

Chapter 10

LOOK, LISTEN, AND HEAL

It was another interesting night in the E.R. We had seen a little bit of everything. The chart I had just been handed belonged to a five-year-old boy who had been experimenting with placing objects in his ear, and his mother caught him in the act. He had been brought in primarily as a punitive measure, I thought, but there was some lingering concern that something might still be in the ear canal. That was where I came in.

I entered the room not knowing what I might find, but the scene proved to be a familiar one. A young, screaming patient, strapped to an exam table, was flanked on all sides by nurses trying their best to restrain him. It had been done for his own good, of course, in an attempt to keep him still, but it wasn't much help. He wasn't going anywhere, but the wiggling, squirming, and fighting had gotten worse.

I begged and pleaded with him to cooperate with me, and I explained exactly what I was trying to do as I inched closer to his little ear. He didn't seem to hear a word I was saying.

After several dozen attempts, I caught little Danny between wiggles and managed to insert the speculum into his small ear canal. "Oh, you've got to be kidding!" I exclaimed. I thought I had seen almost everything a child could put in his ear, but the little guy surprised me. I expected a broken crayon or maybe a piece of candy or a small toy. I once found an unpopped kernel of corn wrapped in an old adhesive bandage. None of that prepared me to deal with Danny's foreign object.

I carefully approached the raisinlike object with the small forceps and attempted a grab at it, but I missed because it moved. Then I realized what a survivor the cockroach is. I momentarily found myself in the midst of a *Star Trek* flashback as I whispered to the nurse, "Good grief, people, I'm a doctor, not an exterminator!" I reached for it one final time, hurriedly closed the forceps, and pulled the wiggling specimen from his ear. "You see this, Danny? *Much* smaller than your elbow, right?" I breathed a deep sigh of relief as I handed it to the nurse and said, "Here, send this down to the lab for proper identification. After all, why should they miss out on all the fun?"

I took a few moments and explained to the parents that the ear would need further medical treatment for the next few days. As Danny was about to hop up from the table, I commented on all the squirming he had done while I was trying to help him. He gave me a puzzled look and said, "Well, you should have told me what you were doing, then I would have been still."

"But, Danny," I replied, "I told you over and over that I needed you to be still. I explained in great detail exactly what I was doing each step of the way. Didn't you hear what I was saying?" Before the question was fully out of my mouth, I noticed a stream of thick material oozing from Danny's ear canal.

Evidence was mounting that his mom had tried several of her own remedies before she had brought him to see us. It seems she had irrigated his ear with hydrogen peroxide, several over-the-counter ear-cleaning solutions, and some thick, smelly gook that looked like a mixture of iodine and old motor oil. I never did figure out what *that* was.

"No wonder you weren't doing what I asked you, Danny. I was speaking right into that ear, and you couldn't hear a thing I was saying, could you?"

"That's what I was trying to tell you," Danny replied. "I didn't know what was happening. That's why I was so scared."

It was an example of a difficult situation made worse by my failure to communicate with Danny. I rubbed my hand across his head and apologized to the little fellow for what had taken place. Then I gave him a coupon for a free hamburger, fries, and a milk shake to enjoy on the way home.

"By the way, Danny . . ."

"Yes, sir?"

"Make sure all that food goes in your mouth, okay?"

As Danny and his parents made their way out the door, I picked up the chart of the next patient. It belonged to an older woman who had fallen only hours earlier and landed awkwardly on her hip. The X ray was already displayed on the view box and revealed a displaced fracture of her proximal femur. Since my physical exam revealed a large amount of soft-tissue swelling in her leg, I was concerned that she was in an unbearable amount of pain.

While I was waiting for the orthopedist to arrive and take her to surgery, I sat down and asked about the details of the accident. I was surprised that through all my questioning, she didn't ask for any medication, especially since the fracture was so severe. Finally, I couldn't stand it any longer. I decided I would ask her if she needed anything to make her more comfortable. She replied that she wasn't really hurting. As I looked at the X ray again, I was certain that at any moment she would begin to feel otherwise, so I ordered a small dose of IV pain medication for her and left to care for other patients.

Within five minutes the nurse came for me. "We need you in trauma six," she said.

"Trauma six . . . that's the woman with the broken hip, isn't it?"

I rushed back into the room to see this petite figure standing up on the stretcher, broken hip and all, while she picked at the multicolored butterflies flitting around her head. As we helped her back into her bed, it occurred to me that the pain medication might have disagreed with her. I was reminded of an old medical axiom: it's very difficult to make a patient feel better if she is not hurting in the first place. If I had truly listened to her, I could have totally avoided the situation.

While I was extinguishing that fire, one of the other E.R. physicians approached and asked to talk with me privately. Once we were isolated in a back corridor, he handed me an EKG tracing and asked, "What do you think about this?"

I glanced at the name on the tracing and recognized it as belonging to Simon, one of our most regular customers. Simon was a harmless enough fellow. He came in when he was bored, complaining of any number of things to get his much-needed dose of attention. Often he required only a sandwich, a few cookies, or a glass of milk to get him moving on his way, but at other times he posed more of a problem. Tonight was one of those times. His complaint was an old standby—persistent indigestion.

"I gave him two of everything we have in the cabinet to treat heartburn and stomach ulcers," my friend told me. "But he kept sitting there, moaning, saying he wasn't feeling any better. I even tried the old ham sandwich routine, but that didn't seem to help, either. Finally, more out of frustration than anything else, I decided to order an EKG. Just look at this!"

I looked at the tracing again. Simon was unmistakably in the midst of having a very real heart attack. "Imagine that," I said. "Simon is actually sick this time. Who would have believed it?"

"Yeah," my friend said. "Who would have believed it? He's been sitting there for almost two hours having a heart attack while I treated him with nothing but antacids and a ham sandwich. What am I supposed to do now?"

I looked through the glass at Simon. He was sitting comfortably on his stretcher. He was obviously in no pain at the moment.

"Well, if it were me," I told him, "I believe I'd explain to Simon exactly what happened, then I'd wipe all that mustard and Maalox off his mouth and call the cardiologist."

Simon did wonderfully that evening, but the incident was a reminder that even the most persistent hypochondriacs eventually have real illnesses. It was another lesson on the value of assuring accurate communication.

Over the years I've learned that when people are in pain, a great service I can offer them is to listen to their complaints. Even at times when there may be no easy solution, it can be therapeutic to verbalize them to someone else. That night was the turning point in the way I approach people's problems. That evening taught me about the importance of communication for anyone who is in the business of trying to help people. Often people who are hurting need something more than a quick fix, a bandage, or a rapid-fire attempt at a cure. Even though it may seem to be a small thing, they all need to be heard and understood. I now see that once I've established an empathetic exchange of communication and shown that I really do care, I can rest assured of one thing: the healing process, however complicated it may be, is already well under way.

Chapter 11

THE MASTERPIECE WITHIN

Jenny was only sixteen years old. She was a little young to be thinking about plastic surgery in my opinion, but that was what she wanted. At least that was what she thought she wanted. The chart said, "Wants to talk about nose job and diet pills." I knew already that the conversation was not going to be easy. It's not that I was unsympathetic to her situation. I remember being sixteen once, long ago, and I knew at that age I didn't want either of those things. But I also knew I hadn't experienced the difficulties that Jenny had faced in her young life. I knew she was dealing with a lot of self-doubt offset by very little self-confidence.

Jenny's life had taken a painful turn when her mother passed away. Three-year-old Jenny and her two sisters were left to be raised by their father, who was rarely at home. Even when he was there, he wasn't much help to them. He was more interested in his own doings than he was in being a parent. The girls lived with him until Jenny was ten, then he departed for greener pastures. "The worst part," Jenny said, "was that he never even said good-bye."

The children were basically abandoned and became wards of the state, little more than numbers in a folder on a social worker's desk. Over the last six years of Jenny's life she had been in and out of numerous foster homes, but only for brief stays in each one. She had begun to believe that no one really wanted her.

Jenny was in search of an identity, in search of a family, but mostly in search of herself. She behaved very politely and always tried to look her best, yet she was not oblivious to the truth. One look in the mirror was enough to remind her that she was no beauty queen. Jenny was learning that adolescence can be a very disturbing time of transition. She was even ready to conclude that she was caught in a phase of the transition that would not end.

Jenny was noticeably overweight, wore braces on her teeth, and had thick eyeglasses. She wasn't really pleased with the size of her nose or the fact that her ears stuck out too far. To further complicate things, she was beginning to wonder if she would ever wear anything but a training bra. She was what we might politely call cosmetically challenged or borderline beauty impaired. Whatever you choose to call it, she wasn't happy with it, and as she was painfully becoming aware, neither were the teenage boys.

"I'm tired of being the shoulder to cry on every time some guy gets dumped by his gorgeous girlfriend," she told me. "Just once I'd like to dump somebody or at least have that option. If I have this surgery, I know all that will change."

Over the next few minutes, I was able to convince her that diet pills and cosmetic surgery were not the solutions to her problems. We talked at length that day and agreed on a program of a reasonable, well-rounded diet, balanced with appropriate exercise and time. She needed time to grow, time to mature, time to let nature take its course.

As she left the office that day, my heart went out to her. I knew she was in pain, feeling the cumulative sting of every insult that had ever been hurled in her direction. I couldn't begin to imagine the taunting she had endured during the difficult developmental period in her life. I knew, however, that it had been substantial. I knew it had motivated her to consider potentially dangerous medication and painful surgery, all in hopes of increasing her popularity among her peers. I just wished I had done a better job of helping her see that her self-worth was not tied inseparably to her physical appearance.

I thought about Jenny several days later as I talked with my neighbor and good friend, Donny Finley. Donny is a renowned painter, an expert artist. Now, I'm the first to admit that my idea of fine art is the picture of the four dogs playing poker, but my wife, who is also an artist, says his work is great, so I decided to have a look. I was expecting to be totally underwhelmed. I was prepared to see abstract blobs of color that look like something any toddler could have done with an ordinary bath sponge. I was also prepared to politely comment that I had been moved by the entire experience, after which I would say thank you and leave. (Call me crazy, but looking at artwork has always seemed to be like taking a big bitter dose of medicine. It isn't really an enjoyable thing to do, but deep down you know it's good for you.)

I must admit, however, I was pleasantly surprised by what I saw. His work really is exceptional! The details were absolutely amazing. We stood for a while and talked about several of his works. Then something interesting struck me. The subjects of many paintings were simple things:

streams or fields or children playing. Several snap-shots on his desk, considerations for future works, also were of rather plain objects, such as an apple or a wildflower. Nothing impressed me as being canvasworthy. (Fortunately, I kept my mouth shut. Art 101 was in session.)

I soon learned that although the things seemed quite ordinary to me, in the eye of the master they were extraordinary. I realized that those blessed with an artistic gift can take what outwardly appears common and find the masterpiece hidden within.

I left his studio pleased with my newfound appreciation for fine art and glad that talented artists can look past the surface and realize where true beauty can be found. They can look at some-thing that most of us would consider as everyday and see in it something rare.

I saw Jenny a couple of weeks later. I was extremely pleased with her progress; her weight was down ten pounds, her exercise tolerance was improved, and her determination to succeed was stronger than ever. The only problem was, she wanted things to go faster. I told her to be patient with herself and continue the good habits she had developed. I told her what I had learned from my neighbor about how an ordinary blank canvas can, with a lot of effort, be transformed into a work of art; about how a beautiful painting can be created from something that might initially seem common; about how a skilled artist can take an object with a rough, unsightly exterior and uncover the masterpiece inside.

"But when?" Jenny asked. "How much longer do I have to wait? I want to be pretty now!" Then her tone suddenly changed. "You're right, of course," she told me. "I guess I've known that all along. And I know it will all be worth it when the day comes. I'm just so anxious for things to be different for me. You can understand that, can't you?"

I smiled, assured her that I fully understood, and reminded her again that these things cannot be rushed.

It's true for each of us. It takes time for the Master Artist to work, to shape, to mold. It takes time to smooth out the rough edges and eventually, when the time is right, to unveil the work of art that was hidden within, the wonderful, *eternal* masterpiece that was there all along.

Chapter 12

REAPING WILD OATS

From all indications, Greg was a young man who had grown up in a family that was much like mine. He was raised in a Christian home by loving parents. Along the way he had made lots of good friends, and for many years he enjoyed a good reputation in his community. But somewhere along the way, around the age of sixteen, things went terribly wrong for Greg.

Greg was a good-looking, very friendly eighteen-year-old, but his life was full of heartache. It was a deep heartache shared by each member of his family.

On his sixteenth birthday he had gotten his first car and along with it his first taste of freedom. It was apparent to everyone that he hadn't used either wisely. He began frequenting the local bars and hanging out with the wrong crowd. Not long afterward Greg made another big mistake when he began dating the wrong kind of girls. Gradually, his old friends lost touch with him.

His parents said he was only "sowing a few wild oats, suffering some growing pains, just going through an awkward stage." *Soon he will grow out of it,* they thought. Then the carousing and the drinking would stop. But they didn't stop. They got worse. The bottle all too easily and all too often becomes the trusted counselor of the troubled teen.

All the warning signs were there. How could they be missed? No one seemed to have the answer to that one, but many other questions were puzzling Greg's parents. Why were his grades suddenly failing? Why didn't he care about his old friends anymore? And where did he go on the nights when he didn't come home at all? Every attempt his family made to reach him failed, and all the while Greg drifted farther and farther away.

Soon he became bored with alcohol alone and began to experiment with other drugs. The story from that point went downhill rapidly. On the night I met Greg, he had had a big argument with his father. It was a continuation of the seemingly never-ending battle for control. The father gave the basic speech we've all heard: "As long as you live under my roof, put your feet under my table, and so on," and it hadn't gone well. His father had tried everything else. He hoped that last resort would bring his son back to him, but it didn't. Greg stormed out of the house, slammed the car door, and sped away, heading to the house of his most recent girlfriend.

He desperately needed to find anyone who would give him a word of support and encouragement. But if he hoped to find that in her, he couldn't have been more disappointed. They, too, began to argue, over money, over his apparent lack of ambition, over the fate of their unborn and still secret child. Once again the words were heated and the exit hasty.

Greg decided he needed to be alone with his one true friend, the only one he knew he could count on to be there without questions, without judgments, without expectations. He turned to his one true escape from reality, and he drank until he literally felt numb. He had learned that there are times when the pain can become so intense that numbness is a welcome alternative.

The next few hours are mostly unaccounted for, but we do know a few things. Despite his intoxicated condition, Greg managed to drive himself into town and park his car outside a run-down building. By that time, he had collected himself enough to locate a fire escape and climb to the top.

That was no small feat, considering it was five stories and he was hardly in complete control of his motor skills.

He sat there alone on the deserted rooftop and continued to drink. Maybe he also began to wonder where he had gone wrong. Maybe he thought about turning his life around. We have no way of knowing, but I do know that he felt very tired and very alone. He was running out of time, needing the support of his family, but turning rather to the demons in the bottle.

As the sun began to rise, someone spotted him up there and, thinking he was a prowler, called the police. By the time they arrived, Greg had wandered dangerously near the building's edge, and he seemed to have every intention of jumping. At such times the suicidal mind reaches the conclusion that there is nothing else to live for. It can be a difficult argument to overcome.

Despite all that, the police were able to initiate a dialogue with Greg. They first tried talking to him about his family, then about his future, but all he could think about was his past. Still, they were optimistic. At times they seemed to make some progress with him, but then he would lose hope and cling to the edge again.

After almost an hour of intense discussion, they were successful in persuading Greg to reconsider what he was doing and come down. He slowly climbed to the bottom of the ladder and jumped a few feet, landing harmlessly on the pavement. Arrangements had been made to take Greg to a local hospital for admission so that he could receive medication and counseling.

One officer said he remembered Greg's comment about being cold just before it happened. Greg calmly reached into his jacket pocket, pulled out a .38 caliber revolver, pushed it into his chest, and squeezed the trigger. Just one shot, that would be sufficient. One shot from the troubled young man, and the deed was done.

"It all happened so fast," I heard one onlooker comment. "There was nothing anyone could have possibly done to stop him."

Standing in the trauma room, I looked at Greg for the first time. He was so very young. I stood at the head of the bed, the surgeon by my side, as we worked furiously to stabilize Greg. Blood was everywhere. Greg's shirt, once beige, was crimson, and the circular hole in his chest continued to remind us that there was much more where that had come from.

The surgeon moved to Greg's side and quickly opened the chest cavity. He spread the ribs with his hands and tried to find anything that would give us cause to be optimistic. Instead, he found that Greg's shot had literally blown a hole right through the center of his heart.

I recalled that I had witnessed some amazing things in the E.R., and I had participated in countless exciting recoveries of trauma victims. For Greg, there would be no heroic retrieval of life from death's doorstep. The outcome was settled before the sound of the blast died away.

I caught the eyes of the surgeon and shook my head, just as he did the same. It had been more than thirty minutes since Greg's arrival, and no pulse or cardiac rhythm had been established. The surgeon stood there, holding Greg's heart in his skilled hands, yet all his attempts to repair it had failed. We had done what we could, but it just wasn't enough. Greg was dead.

X-ray equipment was quickly removed from the room. Glass tubes and rubber gloves were tossed to the floor. IV lines were pulled as their contents, now mixed with Greg's blood, dripped silently to the floor. And the life-sustaining machines that only moments before had blared were hushed in deathly silence.

That's when they found the note Greg had scribbled only hours ago. It was the only clue left to assist in solving the mystery. It was wrinkled, partially torn, and stained with the blood of its author, but it was still legible. It was short, yet disturbingly poignant. Greg wrote, "I don't know what else to do, but I have to find some peace. I'm just really tired of it all." I looked at the body of the young man and realized he would be tired of it all no more. He had found his permanent solution to life's temporary problems.

As I stood reading the note, I heard the cries of anguish down the hall. I knew Greg's family and friends were being informed of what had transpired. I heard the voices of a mother who had lost her firstborn child, a father who had lost his only son. I knew they were left now with only their memories, their grief, and the haunting questions about what might have been if only they had the chance to do things over again.

I knew those were questions Greg's family would ask themselves for the rest of their lives. My questions, however, came from the disturbing note I just read. It continued to play in my mind. Why was he so tired? And where was the peace he searched for, the peace he couldn't seem to find? Greg hadn't found the answer in the bottle. I wondered what might have happened if he had sought counsel somewhere else. I wondered what might have been if Greg had been given one more chance to do things over again.

Later that night I shuffled into my call room with the events of the evening still weighing heavily on my heart. Before lying down for a few moments' rest, I decided to search the Scriptures for an answer, hoping to gain some measure of peace myself. What I found was a verse in Philippians 4 that reminded me where this peace can be found. A peace so perfect and complete that it surpasses my ability to understand it. A peace so wonderful that it can come only from above. I paused and prayed fervently that I would have such a peace. I prayed that one day it would be restored to Greg's family. And somehow, after what I'd seen that night, I knew I would never want to be without it again.

Chapter 13

THE SONG OF DETERMINATION

The stadium was packed with thousands of cheering fans as the runners made their way onto the surface of the track. It was the summer of 1992, and the Olympic Games were in full swing. As usual, there were numerous heartwarming stories to be told. Stories of athletes who had overcome tremendous personal tragedy, great financial hardship, or unbearable political oppression to participate in the Games. But none were as moving as the touching scene the fans were about to witness. They had no way of knowing, but they would remember it for the rest of their lives.

The runners stretched and shook their leg muscles one last time as they carefully dug themselves into the starting blocks. Locked in their sprinter's pose, they waited for the sound of the starter's pistol. It was the sound most of them had waited to hear all their lives. Finally, the gun fired, a wisp of smoke trailed through the air, and the blur of athletes exploded onto the track.

One of the determined faces in that group belonged to a British runner by the name of Derek Redmond. He was a young man at the height of his career, a man who had trained relentlessly to be there, a man who had earned his right to compete for the gold medal. He might not have been heavily favored to win, but he was there. And in the heat of battle, well, who knows? Oftentimes the unexpected happens. And today the unexpected would happen again.

As Redmond was battling for position in the race, he felt a tightening sensation in the back of his leg. At first he tried to dismiss it, but soon the pain became so great that he could ignore it no longer. On the biggest day of his athletic career, Redmond experienced a serious hamstring injury. It was obvious to those in person as well as to the international TV audience that the physical pain was surpassed only by the emotional disappointment he was having to endure.

I remember watching the conclusion of the contest and seeing the pack of runners dash onward, leaving the injured sprinter in their wake. As the race was ending, I assumed Redmond had hobbled over to the sideline for medical attention, but he had not. Moments later the camera was back on Redmond again, but he wasn't collapsed on the infield grass in the care of his trainer. Amazingly, he was still in his lane, hopping on one leg toward the finish line. He was in pain. He was in tears. But he was determined to do what he had set out to do. He had come to the Olympics to run his best, and he refused to leave without the knowledge and satisfaction that he had done just that.

After several more yards of hopping toward the goal, it became evident that the pain was increasing. All eyes were fixed on the young man, watching intently, hoping he would make it, yet wondering how he could. There was still such a long way to go, and he was losing strength with each second. But he would not have to go the rest of his journey alone. From the stands a figure rushed onto the track and, against all Olympic regulations, ran over to give support to the ailing warrior.

Redmond offered no resistance. He put his arm around the man, and the two of them hobbled together toward the finish line. Security guards made their way toward them and tried to explain that such assistance was not permitted, but they were brushed aside. The man who was helping the hurting athlete, Redmond's father, held him even tighter and told him they could make it. As they neared the end of the race, the father was heard to say, "We started this thing together. We're going to finish it together."

Redmond didn't win the race that day. He had no place on the podium, no medal to place around his neck, but the cheers he heard from the crowd were greater than for any of the victors. For Redmond himself was truly a victor. He fought through the tears and the pain and refused to quit when many would have. Redmond made it to the finish line.

There are so few times in our lives when we encounter someone with such determination and such strong will. But I have seen others. And though most are not Olympic athletes, they have, nonetheless, inspired those who have watched them. They have reminded us all of the importance of staying in the game and finishing the race. One such story involves a person I've known for most of my life: a young woman named LaJuan.

On December 16, 1959, a wonderfully healthy baby girl was brought into this world. After much thought her parents decided on the name LaJuan, a beautiful name for such a beautiful little girl. She appeared to be developing normally and passed her six-week checkup with flying colors. The family had big dreams for their young child, but only two days later, their dreams would be shattered and their hopes for the future altered in a way they never could have imagined.

On Saturday morning as they were making a routine trip to run some errands, they were hit head-on by a drunken driver. LaJuan's mother and father were both seriously injured and were taken, in their unconscious condition, to a nearby hospital for treatment. Moments later, strictly by chance, LaJuan's grandmother happened by and recognized the crumpled car. She was brought to tears as she saw the extent of the accident and learned the nature of the injuries. She was told that two adults, both in serious condition, had just been taken away by ambulance.

"But what about the baby?" she asked the rescue personnel. "Who's taking care of her?"

Unfortunately, no one knew anything about the baby. The emergency crew immediately began searching through what was left of the car. That was when they found her. LaJuan was lying in the floorboard of the backseat, barely alive, covered by some clothes that were destined for the cleaners. Her tiny skull was shattered in three places, her chest was crushed, and her pulses were only faintly palpable. The drunken fellow, by the way, was sound asleep in his car, having suffered a nasty scratch on his forehead.

The critically injured baby was taken to the

same E.R. as her parents, but she was given little hope for survival. The parents, who were now recovering, were told there was almost no chance she would live. She had suffered too much damage. There was nothing they could do but wait to see what happened, wait to see if she was strong enough to survive.

LaJuan would laugh about that statement later. You see, it was just the first of many times her strength would be called into question. But each time the question was raised, she responded with a resounding *yes.*

Three weeks following the accident, much to the surprise of the physicians, LaJuan was still stubbornly fighting for her life. Since she had made it that far, the doctors determined that she might benefit from surgery to open her cranial cavity. It was the only hope of removing the blood that was clotted and pressing on her brain. Somehow she survived the surgery, and within hours she was opening her eyes and searching the room for her mother. It was a remarkable story of courage even if it had ended here, but three months later LaJuan was still battling to live. Not only was she alive—she was steadily improving.

The surgeons once again approached her parents and told them she would need another operation. A shunt would have to be placed to relieve the brain of the excess buildup of fluid. They had hoped it would not be necessary, and in all honesty they hadn't thought she would survive long enough to need it. But she *had* survived.

The risks, of course, were great. Such a small child. Such a complicated surgery.

"Fifty-fifty. That's the best odds I can give you," the surgeon told them. "But I'll guarantee you that without it, her odds are much worse. Without it, her odds are zero."

The only reason anyone could give for her surviving the surgery was her unyielding determination to live. There was just no other way to explain it. Still, there were many concerns over her ability to function after such a complex operation. Even if she did survive, the doctors told them, she would certainly be severely retarded. It was unlikely she would ever hear or speak, and certainly, she would never walk without assistance. To make matters worse, they were told that what little vision she had would also likely be severely impaired. They were told she would never live to see the age of two.

But at her two-year checkup, the attitude of the physicians slowly began to change. As the doctors thoroughly examined LaJuan, they could do little but shake their heads in amazement.

"And what medicine does she take?" one of them asked her mother.

But LaJuan interrupted. "All I'm taking is phenobarbital," she answered.

After that statement, there were no more predictions about her survival. The young girl had astounded them all. And she wasn't through yet.

When LaJuan reached the age of six, with no valid reason not to do it, her parents decided to enroll her in school. LaJuan absolutely loved it, and in all honesty she began to catch on quickly. (Believe me, I know. She sat right next to me.) Shortly thereafter her father passed away unexpectedly, but she would not use that as an excuse to quit. She had come too far. She recovered from the loss and eventually went back to school.

LaJuan's medical problems, however, were far from over. Over the next few years she had many more surgeries. Some of them were expected procedures to repair or replace the shunt. Others were unexpected, due to falls or other injuries. But through it all the wonderful little girl never gave up hope. After one particular emergency surgery, the physician entered the room and explained that it had been a little more difficult than he had anticipated.

"To tell you the truth," he told LaJuan's mother, "I was afraid for a while that we had lost her."

LaJuan responded in her typical fashion. Still groggy from the effects of the anesthesia, she took the hand of her surgeon and said, "Doctor, I was never worried for a minute. I always knew I was going to make it."

"Well, honey," he replied, "next time be sure and tell me."

Someone once approached LaJuan's mother and asked, "How does LaJuan do it? How does she manage to overcome such adversity and maintain such a positive attitude?"

"That's simple," she said. "When LaJuan is in pain, she just sings."

Singing spiritual songs has always been a big part of her life. Sometimes she will sit alone for hours singing of heaven, of God and His angels.

"It just seems that the singing gives her life purpose," her mother says. "It's a way for her to ignore the difficulties and focus on something positive. She first learned of the healing power of her songs when she was on her way to Memphis to see an orthopedic specialist. LaJuan had fallen and severely broken her hip. She made the long trip lying in the backseat of the car, surrounded on all sides by pillows. Still, any movement, even the slightest jarring, greatly increased her pain. Even the medication offered no relief. Finally, she just started singing.

"After a few moments I looked into the backseat to see tears streaming down both of her cheeks, but there was still a smile on her face. That was the first time she told me, 'Mom, even if the pills don't do anything to help with the pain, the singing about God sure does.'"

Since that time LaJuan has suffered other fractures due to the weakness of her bones. At the age of twenty-two, LaJuan was forced to begin using a wheelchair. She never really wanted to do it, but the risk of falling and the pain she was enduring had become too great. Still, she never lost her determination. She never let her condition get the best of her.

Recently, I went back home and had the opportunity to visit with LaJuan. I hadn't seen her in some time, yet I knew her condition had deteriorated somewhat due to her chronic arthritis and the old fractures. I really can't explain why I was amazed at what took place; by now I should have learned to expect it. LaJuan stood from the sofa and walked over to hug me. It seems that after fifteen long years she decided she had grown tired of her metallic companion, and she had pushed her wheelchair aside. Despite concern from the family and numerous warnings from her physicians, LaJuan devised and implemented her own personal plan of physical therapy. She worked hard for months at home alone, building and strengthening her muscles. When her doctors realized she would not take no for an answer, she was referred to a physical therapist and literally learned to walk all over again. She is still walking to this day for one reason: she is determined to do so. She simply refuses to give up.

And if you have the privilege of visiting with her in her home, you will likely find her studying her Bible. She might also be doing some knitting for a friend, and you will probably even hear her singing a hymn or two. But one thing you won't want to miss is that old wheelchair sitting over in the corner of her room. It's abandoned, with no other purpose than to gather dust and serve as a conversation piece. I have strong personal suspicions that's exactly where it will stay. And somewhere in heaven there are angels working overtime to prepare an extra special place for this wonderfully inspiring soul. A place where there will be no more pain, but lots of singing. A place where she can walk without the fear of falling. A place where the surgeon's knife will never touch her again.

In fact, I feel certain that each day when she talks to the Father, she hears Him say, "I know you can make it. Just hang in there a little longer. We started this thing together. We're going to finish it together."

Chapter 14

TREASURE FOUND

It was April 18, 1989. I had been in the labor and delivery room all night, but I had rested briefly. The young woman actually doing the work, the one in labor, had not slept at all. Loud monitors, noisy intercoms, and frequent painful contractions had seen to that. It was a difficult and very uncertain time for her. Her IV line was leaking, her epidural block had failed hours ago, and it seemed as though her baby would never arrive. She was understandably anxious and scared. She looked to me for encouragement and silently hoped that everything would be okay. It was 8:00 A.M.

By noon, precious little progress had been made. We began to entertain thoughts that a C-section might be necessary, but only time would tell, so we waited. At 1:00 P.M., we decided on an attempt to deliver the baby with the aid of forceps. If that was unsuccessful, we would be forced to proceed with the C-section.

Just as the delivery attempt was under way, signs of mild fetal distress were beginning to appear on the monitor. Time was of the essence. Some tense moments followed, but the forceps attempt worked, and a beautiful, healthy baby girl was brought into this world. As I assisted in caring for the newborn, I was overcome with the sense of new life from such simple beginnings. But the baby was no ordinary child. The baby was special because she was mine.

I looked at my wife, exhausted from long labor, but glowing as only a new mother can, and I knew we had been given a precious gift. We had been entrusted by God to care for the new being, the utterly helpless and dependent soul. I realized at that moment that life is very valuable, something to treasure.

Exactly six years later, I sat across the table from my child and marveled at how she had grown. It was her birthday dinner, and she wanted filet mignon. "Why not?" I said. "You turn six only one time."

"Tell me the story about how I was born, Daddy!" she asked over dinner. She smiled widely as she heard the complicated tale once again. She had long been convinced that no matter how much trouble it had been, she was worth it. I looked at that smile on her face, short by a couple of front teeth, and knew she was right.

I watched my wife cutting the steaks for her and our son, Christopher. Crayons were scattered everywhere and stuffed animal fur had found its way into my salad, but it was good anyway. I wouldn't have missed that dinner for the world. The kids left the restaurant wearing more steak than they had eaten, yet they had had a good time, and that was what was important.

After returning home, I turned on the news while we dressed the kids for bed. We learned of a horrible accident that had just occurred. A navy jet was flying from the Carolinas to Texas when it experienced engine failure. An emergency landing attempt was unsuccessful, and it crashed in a nearby county. All eight passengers were lost. We watched as rescue crews sifted through the wreckage for bodies, and I hugged my children tightly. I was again reminded of the value of life, and of our treasure.

The next day was business as usual. With the last piece of birthday cake carefully packed into Lindsay's lunchbox, I dropped her off at school and headed for the office. It was ironic that Jim was the first patient I saw that day. He was back for a recheck of his blood pressure medication, and he had been doing well.

"Been on the pills about six months now," he said. His blood pressure was great; no side effects were noted. As I thumbed through his chart, I noticed that the last time I saw him was after his own accident.

Jim was in the army reserve, having served our country well for nearly twenty-five years. Six months ago, he and his deputy commander were on a routine helicopter flight when they, too, experienced mechanical difficulty. The tail mechanism of the aircraft failed, rendering them unable to guide and unable to land the helicopter. The pilots responded quickly and heroically as the aircraft fell approximately six hundred feet in less than ten seconds. After the "controlled crash" as he called it, Jim started to throw open the door to exit, but for some reason he stopped. "Good thing I did," he said. The blades were turned so badly that they would most likely have taken off his head. The helicopter was barely recognizable as such, but all five passengers exited without injury.

"It was a miracle," Jim said. "Nobody could believe that such a crash could be survived by anyone, much less the entire crew. We were all very fortunate that day." The pilot in charge was recommended for the Broken Wing Award, one rarely given. It's reserved for pilots who have done something so amazing that it can be thought of only as miraculous. Two other crew members were also nominated for awards, and through it all, no argument was heard from Jim. He knew they were well deserved.

As he finished recounting the incident, I asked him what had gone through his mind during those few moments as they fell helplessly toward the earth. Had his life flashed before him? Had he thought something profound?

"No, not really," he said. "To tell you the truth, I didn't think anything like that. My only thought was, *I'm going to die here with these people,* and that really made me reconsider some things. You know, I'd always thought in a situation like that, I might say a prayer or at least think of God. But I didn't, and it bothered me. I thought, *If I didn't turn to God at a time like that, what was I waiting for?* It was afterward that I decided to make some changes in my life, to get my ducks in a row with the Man upstairs. I realized that I needed to spend more time with my wife, with my two girls. I decided work would no longer be the most important thing to me. I would devote myself to God and then to my family."

I was impressed with his honesty and with his wisdom. He had been granted a second chance, and he was determined to make the most of it. I knew that Jim, too, had been reminded of the value of life, and of his treasure. We talked for a moment about the unfortunate crash of the navy jet the night before, and I could tell he felt for them more keenly than I did. That was understandable. After all, he had been there. I hadn't.

I thought about a verse of Scripture I'd heard many times in the past, but never had it seemed more relevant than it did at that moment. A statement found in James 4 compares life to a mist that appears only for a moment, then vanishes as quickly as it came. Never had my existence seemed more like a mist than it did that morning.

I talked to Jim a few more minutes, then he left the office. I felt, however, that I knew more about him than when he had entered. I knew more than just a blood pressure reading or a test result. I knew about his character, and I knew that his family was in good hands.

Preparing to enter the next patient's room, I saw some of our staff with tears in their eyes, huddled around a radio. They told me that someone had parked a van full of explosives outside the federal building in Oklahoma City. The result was devastating. Such senseless killing. Such horrible loss. But a reminder to those of us who remain that our lives truly are but a mist, here briefly, then gone.

I watched the news that night, as did all of you, and I was terrified by what I saw. I was overcome simultaneously by a sense of compassion and a sense of helplessness as I watched body after body, young and old, being pulled from the crumbled remains of the building. Although I couldn't do anything to help those people, I knew what I could do.

I've held my wife and children in my arms a little more tightly than usual since that day. I've also enjoyed our trips to the park a little bit more, and for some reason, spilled juice doesn't seem to bother me as much as it used to. I realize that each day I have with my family is something very precious. And once again I am reminded of the value of life, and of my treasure.

Chapter 15

KEEP IT SIMPLE, PLEASE

Maggie had never seen the inside of a hospital, not before today. It was her first trip into the hallowed halls of medicine, and it would prove to be a memorable one. She was an intriguing woman of seventy-one years, the mother of seven children, all born at home.

Maggie had gotten up early that morning and gone about her usual routine of cooking breakfast for the family. She noticed her ankles were more swollen than usual, but she gave them no further thought. Some mild shortness of breath occurred soon afterward, followed by chest pain, then by fear.

An ambulance was called, and she was brought to the emergency room suffering from severe respiratory distress. The look in her eyes was that of impending doom, yet she was too short of breath to tell us anything. An electrocardiogram was done to rule out a possible heart attack, but it was normal. Her chest X ray was not nearly so consoling. She was in pulmonary edema, a condition where fluid accumulates in the lungs, making breathing nearly impossible. Her arterial oxygen level confirmed that she was in real danger. Whatever we were going to do had to be done quickly.

Since she was obviously very frightened, we made every effort to calm her while I placed a breathing tube in her airway. The ventilator support with high-dose oxygen proved to be just what she needed, and subsequent blood oxygen levels showed significant improvement in her respiratory function.

The next step was to manipulate her volume status with the use of strong diuretics. It was only after eighty milligrams of IV Lasix that she began ridding herself of the excess fluid that had caused her to be so short of breath and threatened to take her life. Never is the sight of a rapidly filling catheter bag more attractive than in a critically ill patient with pulmonary edema. She immediately began feeling better. She was still very frightened, but also very cooperative. She realized she had to trust me if she wanted to survive.

Shortly after her transfer from the E.R. to the

intensive care unit, her condition began to stabilize. Over the next several days I continued gradually removing the fluid from her body with the use of the diuretics, and Maggie slowly started regaining her strength. Since there was no evidence of heart damage, I was able to get her off the ventilator rather quickly, much to her approval. Two days spent choking on a large plastic tube in your throat would be enough to try anyone's patience, and Maggie was no exception. She was more than ready to have it taken out. I carefully deflated the cuff on the tube, then slowly pulled the lifesaving, yet painful device from her trachea. She was still scared, but also grateful as I heard her speak for the first time.

"I thought I was going to die with that tube in my mouth!" she said, still coughing from its irritating effect. She thoroughly wiped her mouth and face with a washcloth and tried to regain her composure.

"Am I going to be okay now? What on earth happened to me?" she asked.

Only then did I realize that Maggie had absolutely no idea what had transpired over the last forty-eight hours. She had been an unwilling passenger on a confusing and sometimes horrifying ride on the intensive care roller coaster. It was obviously a trip she never wanted to take again.

Granted, the complex world of medicine had just spared her life, but it had also totally overwhelmed her in the process.

I tried to explain in detail what I had done, why I had done it, and what I would likely need to do in the next few days. She still looked puzzled, but she knew two things for sure: (1) she was very sick when she arrived, and (2) she was much better now. Maggie hesitated with her decision, then cautiously agreed to abide by my suggestions. Her improvement continued, and less than one week from her emergency admission, she was ready for discharge.

Prior to her leaving I sat with her, carefully reviewed her medications, and scheduled a return visit for follow-up in three weeks. As it turned out, however, I would see her sooner than that.

Approximately two weeks after her release, I received a frantic message from the clinic nurse. "Maggie is here, and she says it feels like something is sticking in her chest!" I was involved in another emergency situation at the time and couldn't leave right away, so I ordered an EKG and chest X ray to be performed. I assured the nurse I would be there as soon as I could.

On the way to the clinic, I was already making mental arrangements to have Maggie readmitted to the hospital. I feared another episode of respiratory distress had occurred, possibly complicated by some serious cardiac damage. I knew we had narrowly dodged the bullet last time; this time I feared we would not be so fortunate.

I rushed into the clinic, grabbed the chart, and threw open the exam room door, startling Maggie. I must have looked equally startled because what I saw was not at all what I had expected. Maggie appeared calm and comfortable lying there, relaxing on the exam table, totally absorbed in a magazine. Her X ray was displayed on the view box next to her, and much to my surprise, it was perfectly normal. Her EKG also showed no cause for concern.

"Glad you finally got here, Doc," she said. "I almost fell asleep waiting."

Convinced serious danger was afoot, I blurted out, "Tell me about this sticking pain you have in your chest, Maggie."

"What pain?" she replied. "I'm not having any pain. I told the nurse I have something that's sticking on my chest."

As she said that, she lifted her shirt, and there the little culprit was, just beneath her left breast. It was a small circular adhesive pad that had been applied during her admission, used to monitor her heart while in intensive care. It had been there since her discharge. She had bathed around it, dressed around it, even reapplied it on one occasion when it almost fell off. She had been very careful not to disturb its position for fear of compromising its effectiveness.

I fought back a grin and quietly wished I could convince some of my other patients to take such interest in their medications. I didn't have the heart to tell her that it had been left by mistake and was absolutely of no benefit. I decided to compliment her on having taken such good care of it. I then remarked, truthfully, that I couldn't recall ever having had a patient care for one so well. I assured her, however, that it had fulfilled its purpose and could now be safely removed. I took extra care as I painstakingly peeled it from her fragile skin. She smiled, thanked me, and left the office.

I was again reminded that Maggie was totally lost in our world of high-tech medical gadgetry. All the big words and fancy machines were more than her untrained mind could understand, so she had to trust me with the faith of an innocent child.

A few weeks later I got a glimpse of how Maggie might have felt in my world of medicine: confused, possibly bewildered, maybe a little overwhelmed. It happened, oddly enough, in the middle of a worship service. One Sunday morning

I tried to imagine what my perception would have been if it were my first time in such a setting. If I knew nothing whatsoever about religion. If I'd never heard the story of the Bible, never had much use for Christians, and never seen the inside of a church building before that day.

I must admit, the singing was absolutely beautiful. The words spoke to me of "cherubim and seraphim" and something about a "night with ebon pinion." Oh, it was impressive. And the speaker was equally dramatic. It was a wonderful discourse on the scriptural authenticity of various biblical translations, compared, I think, to some Greek person. I assure you, it was very moving.

With my experiment concluded, I headed for the back of the building to pick up my two children, who were busy in their training hour. They had their own little message, something about caring for each other, about loving our neighbors. And then they sang.

I was reminded that day of the trust I had seen in Maggie's face because I witnessed it again in the faces of those children as they listened to the uncomplicated teaching of our Lord. And I heard it in the simple message contained in their beautiful singing as they lifted their angelic voices and told me,

Jesus loves me! this I know,
For the Bible tells me so.
Little ones to Him belong,
They are weak but He is strong.
Yes, Jesus loves me!
Yes, Jesus loves me!
Yes, Jesus loves me!
The Bible tells me so.

Chapter 16

THE ANGEL IN THE NURSERY

Nathan had his own little baby bed in the corner of the pediatric nursery. It was very cute, decorated with cars, teddy bears, and horses. It was the only home he had ever known. His parents were young, poor, and unmarried. They chose not to assume the responsibility of rearing a child. One day when Nathan was two months old, they visited with him for a few minutes, then left. No one at the hospital had seen them since. Letters were mailed, but returned with no forwarding address. Social workers visited, but no one was ever home. The phone number on the chart had long been disconnected. With no reason to believe the parents would ever return, little Nathan's future was in the hands of the courts.

Nathan was born with significant medical problems, the most serious of which stemmed from his premature arrival. He weighed only three pounds at birth and had such underdeveloped lungs that his chances for survival looked very grim. But he was a fighter. He beat the odds and lived. During his complicated delivery, Nathan had also suffered a fractured collarbone and a dislocated hip, but those were only minor obstacles for him. He overcame them quickly.

Even though he was improving, he needed several weeks of treatment in the pediatric intensive care unit following his birth. Much to our delight, he responded extremely well to the medications and steadily gained strength every day. Soon, he was ready to do what no one thought he would ever be able to do. He was ready to breathe without the assistance of the ventilator. He began breathing like an old pro and soon moved to the regular nursery. It was a joyous occasion for all the staff. There was even a small party with a cake made by a nurse. Everyone was glad to see him doing so well. It was such a shame his parents weren't around to celebrate, too.

In the regular nursery, Nathan's treatment remained complex. A catheter had been placed in his bladder due to some problems in his urinary tract. It required close supervision and constant nursing care. To further complicate things, he developed asthma and required frequent breathing treatments. But everyone, it seemed, enjoyed caring for Nathan. Everyone, that is, except his parents.

As Nathan continued to thrive, the hospital was in somewhat of a dilemma. It was apparent that no one knew exactly what to do with Nathan. Oh, everyone loved having him around, but the long-term issues were yet to be decided. Could he be placed in a foster home? Would he possibly be adopted? Would his parents ever return and try to regain custody? Through all the discussions, the precious little fellow stayed where he was in the corner bed of the pediatric nursery.

I was an intern when I first met Nathan. His story touched my heart and that of everyone who met him. By that time, Nathan was eighteen months old with golden blonde hair and dark brown eyes. But I most remember his smile. He had a trusting, heartwarming smile.

I noticed something else about Nathan as I became more familiar with him. I knew it was something I could never prove, but I began to sense his loneliness. It wasn't something he could tell you—he had spoken very few words—but you could sense it. Even with all the caring nurses, adoring residents, and attentive staff, he knew something was different about his life. Make no mistake about it, even the smallest children can feel the pain of abandonment. Every moment without a nurturing mother, without a loving father, Nathan had felt it.

He tried to make the best of his situation, but it was obvious he wanted desperately to belong to somebody. What he wanted most was the one thing we couldn't give him: the love of his very own parents.

He thrived on attention. Every time someone walked into the nursery, his eyes lit up. He jumped to his feet and held up his little arms, wanting to be loved even if only for a little while.

One day two of my fellow interns and I took Nathan on a tour of the hospital. We took him to lunch, went for a walk on the grass, even had his picture made and placed on his own hospital I.D. badge. He absolutely loved it. From that day on he wore the badge religiously. It was one of very few things in this world he could call his own.

I thought about Nathan many times that year. I often visited him even after the pediatrics rotation ended. No matter how difficult things had been, spending a few minutes with him gave me a fresh perspective. Trouble was, it was getting harder and harder to see him. Sometimes I visited when a line of people wanted to talk to him, play with him, or just hold him. People went out of their way to be nice to him because he was so sweet, but also because they felt such sympathy for him. It was such a sad situation to be so young and so alone.

I couldn't imagine what it was like to grow up as an orphan. I have so many fond memories of good times with my brother and sister and my parents. I often wondered how emotionally devastating the situation might be for Nathan, especially if he grew up thinking that no one wanted him. I hoped soon that the legal entanglements would be settled, and Nathan would be able to have a real home. I hoped he wouldn't grow up feeling abandoned.

Then one day I went by to see him just to say hello, but he was gone. "Some nice family," the nurses said. They had picked him up just two days before. I was sad I hadn't gotten to say good-bye, but I was also excited for Nathan. I was glad he had taken the first step toward having a normal life. I could picture his room full of stuffed animals, toys and dolls, and his own big bed. But he would have something much more important than all that. He would have his own identity and the love of his very own parents. No one deserved it more than he did; it was what he always wanted.

Not long ago I was searching through the cable channels when I ran across an interview with the heavyweight fighter George Foreman. It was a lively discussion as they talked about his boxing career, his business exploits, and his world-famous appetite. Near the end of the conversation, however, things began to get more serious. One of the last questions was about Mr. Foreman's family, specifically why he named all of his sons George. I was expecting another one of his humorous responses. I thought he named them all George because of some ego insufficiency or maybe because of his flamboyant nature. But that wasn't the case at all.

His tone became sober when he said he had grown up in a broken home, never really knowing his father. The other kids constantly ridiculed him, but worst of all was his doubt about not knowing who he really was. It was amazing to hear about his struggle for identity, especially considering the outgoing personality he has now. But growing up without a dad can be difficult, he said, and it was something he was determined would never happen to any of his boys. That's why he named them all after himself. They may go by different nicknames, but make no mistake about it, they are all George Foreman. And now, no matter where they are, no matter how tough the times, they know they have a father who loves them and cares for them and who wanted them enough to give them his own name. That was his special gift to each of them.

It was certainly an interesting story, but as I

turned off the television I realized it was hardly an original one. I remembered that regardless of the status of our earthly family, each of us is the recipient of that same special gift. Each of us has a heavenly Father who made that same commitment to us. And as gifts go, it just doesn't get any better than that.

Chapter 17

ETERNITY'S DOOR

The cardiologist peered at me over his bifocals, shook his head, and bluntly remarked, "This is not good." He was looking at the films of Evelyn's heart he had just done during an emergency arteriogram. He threw his heavy lead apron over a nearby chair, walked closer to the video screen, and began pointing out all the culprit lesions in her arteries. The pictures required no explanation. The blockages were so advanced they would have been obvious to a casual observer, but he felt compelled to enumerate them for me, so I stood and listened.

"Not much we can do here," he told me. "Do you want me to talk to her?"

"Better let me do it," I said. "I've known her for a long time. It'll be better coming from me." I entered the stairwell and headed for the unit to fulfill my difficult task.

In the coronary care unit, Evelyn was resting in

her bed, surrounded by her five loving children and about a dozen noisy machines. She was a sweet seventy-two-year-old who had been tending to her usual affairs that day when her activities were rudely interrupted by sharp, stabbing chest pains. I pushed back the curtain and sat at Evelyn's feet, wondering how I would explain to her and her family that her life would soon be over.

Evelyn had just suffered a serious heart attack, her third, but this one was clearly the worst. The last one was less than a year ago, followed by open heart surgery and months of rehabilitation. Three grafts had been placed to reroute the flow of blood around the clogged arteries in an attempt to save her precious heart muscle. Three grafts, four weeks of hospitalization, and months of suffering all to no avail. Those grafts now were clotted and nonfunctional, as were all of her native vessels. The damage this time had destroyed most of the pumping ability left in her aging heart. No surgery would be of benefit at this point; no last-minute clot-dissolving drugs could save her now.

"I'm very sorry," I told them, "but I've just reviewed her angiography films with the cardiologist, and there isn't anything we can salvage. There has been too much damage."

With the function of her heart badly compromised I knew she could survive no more than a matter of hours. The fluid was accumulating around her lungs so quickly that she required frequent doses of diuretics to enable her to breathe. The nurses shuffled in and out quietly as I continued my explanation. They, too, knew the battle would soon be over.

"I have to be honest with you," I told them. "We'll do everything we can, but she is opposed to being on the ventilator, and with the loss of so much heart muscle it's unlikely she'll make it through the night." Her children stood before me in shock, and their eyes filled with tears as they tried to absorb the news.

The hospital chaplain was called, and the family was taken to a conference room to wait while we worked with the precious soul who was critically ill. I stood at her bedside and continued my attempts to stabilize Evelyn. Even as I did, I noticed from the corner of my eye several irregular heartbeats on her cardiac monitor. She was beginning to experience short runs of ventricular tachycardia, a life-threatening rhythm abnormality. It was an ominous sign, but hardly unexpected. I ordered a loading dose of lidocaine and began a continuous drip in an attempt to stop the sinister beats, but it was soon apparent that would not be effective.

Barely had the medication been started when

Evelyn became hypotensive, pale, and pulseless. I looked again to her monitor, which revealed ventricular fibrillation. Alarms sounded throughout the unit as the nurse handed me the defibrillator paddles and stood clear. The electrical shock immediately restored her to a normal rhythm and brought a look of bewilderment to her now conscious eyes. I watched as she grabbed her chest with both hands and began crying softly. I was astonished at how quickly she recovered, and I promptly apologized for hurting her.

Over the next twenty minutes Evelyn required defibrillation three more times. Finally, she looked at me with weary eyes, told me how painful that was, and asked me if I would please stop. I feared what would happen if I did, but I refused to hurt her anymore. Reluctantly, I agreed, and the defibrillator was removed from the room. Moments later another episode of V-fib occurred. I instinctively gave a gentle thump to her chest, and with the lidocaine in her system, she again returned to a normal rhythm. Her pulses, however, were becoming noticeably weaker. With no other alternative, I began light chest compressions, and much to my surprise she again regained consciousness.

I explained to her what had happened and why the compressions were necessary. She smiled weakly and thanked me. Evelyn's heart was near the end of its long journey. Each beat brought the aged muscle closer to the finish line. Every time I tried to discontinue the compressions, she slipped from consciousness. When the compressions restarted, she slowly awakened and began talking to me again. I know she sensed my bewilderment, but I honestly had never witnessed anyone linger so long at the door that separates life from death.

After that pattern continued for some time, I told Evelyn there was nothing else I could do for her. Even in her deteriorating condition she understood exactly what I meant. She realized once the compressions ceased she would soon be gone.

That's when I asked her the question. I'm not really sure why I asked it, maybe for lack of anything better to say. Nevertheless, I looked into her eyes that were so near death and asked if there was anything she wanted to say to anyone before I stopped. She smiled and said, "Yes, I would like to say good-bye to my children if that's okay." I assured her it was.

The nurses took a few moments to prepare the family for what they were about to see and quietly escorted them back to the bedside of their dying mother. Evelyn began to cry as they filed in, and she called them each by name for the last time. She told them to remember that she loved them and that she would miss them. She charged them with strict instructions regarding her grandchildren, hugged them all one final time, then watched as they left the room.

As I stood over her with only the nurses present, we, too, said our good-byes to Evelyn. It had been an emotional experience for all of us. Evelyn reached for my hand, thanked me for what we had done, and closed her eyes to rest. Her last words were unintelligible to me, but I was sure they were uttered in prayer. With her lips silent, I slowly stopped the rhythmic compressions on her frail chest and watched as she drifted off to sleep. Moments later she was pronounced dead.

I regained my composure as best I could, crossed the hall to the conference room, and talked with the family for quite a while. I told them she had gone peacefully, and I reminded them that she would no longer suffer. They thanked me and commented that she had been ready to go for a long time.

I slept very little that night. I kept thinking about the scene at Evelyn's bedside, a loving mother sharing a tearful good-bye with her adoring children. And it occurred to me that her final request, to talk one last time to her family, would have been my final request as well. It was something I did every day, but it seemed more important that night.

I thought about the other tasks I had performed that day—calling for bank balances, paying the mortgage, checking the stock market, reading the newspaper. Still, I couldn't get off my mind the fact that Evelyn seemed totally unconcerned about such matters, opting to spend a few final moments with her children.

But I learned one final thing about Evelyn that night. Before I could leave the conference room, one of her sons had a final question for me.

"She had a calm look on her face in there, didn't she, Doc? Did you notice it?"

"I sure did," I replied.

"I knew she would. I really did," he told me. "She's always been at peace with herself, at peace with all of us, and at peace with God."

He was right. The look was unmistakable. And I knew she had passed into eternity with the peaceful understanding that those relationships had made all the difference in her life.

Chapter 18

PEARLS BEFORE SWINE

It was Christmas Eve, almost bedtime, and the excitement on the faces of my children was payment enough for each moment spent in those long lines over the last few weeks. But such a level of anticipation also carried a downside. No matter how hard they tried, they couldn't seem to fall asleep. If the truth be known, at the ages of five and three, they weren't totally at ease with the idea of a large stranger in a red suit roaming around our house in the middle of the night. So, for those and numerous other reasons, they were allowed to sleep in our bed that night.

Once they were fast asleep I crept out of the room to take care of a few jobs of my own. My primary responsibility was to act as an assistant to Santa's elves and deal with the three most ominous words known to humankind: *some assembly required.* I worked at a feverish pace and attempted to test the accuracy of my theory that with the aid of a large enough hammer part A will always fit into part B. Hours later, with my knuckles bruised and bleeding and my faith in God adequately tested, I slumped back into bed for a few hours of rest.

Around five o'clock, however, I received a rather rude wake-up call. Deb was intent on maximizing the kids' Christmas experience, even to the point of getting up at a ridiculous hour to ring a few jingle bells and rattle a paper sack in the next room. She was creating the mental picture of Santa walking around the house as he unloaded his sack full of goodies. Now if you've ever considered trying to trick your children in this fashion, take this opportunity to learn from our mistake. It really isn't worth the embarrassment.

After the ringing and rattling had gone on for about twenty minutes, Lindsay woke up, bolted straight up in bed, and said, "Daddy, do you hear that?"

Trying my best to feign sleep, I mumbled, "What do you think you hear?"

"Those jingle bells, Daddy. Don't you hear them?"

Then she suddenly began crying.

"What's wrong, honey? Why are you crying?"

"Because, Daddy, we waited all night for Santa Claus and he finally came and now Mommy's going to scare him away if she doesn't quit rattling that grocery bag and come back to bed."

As I said, it really isn't worth the embarrassment. Children are just too smart nowadays.

I guess we've all had those moments, haven't we? We tried to pull a fast one on somebody and got caught red-handed. About the only feeling worse than that is having someone pull a fast one on us and get away with it. Believe me, I know. It happened not long ago to me. The worst of it is, I consider myself to be somewhat perceptive. But Michael really had me going for a few days.

I was very tired that particular night. I was just about to leave the clinic and head for home, but that shrill mechanical sound interrupted the silence and destroyed my plans for the evening. The harsh, unmistakable sound of my ear-piercing electronic leash was calling me to the hospital. I had just been consulted to see Michael in the emergency room.

Michael seemed to be a healthy enough fellow, about forty years of age by my first guess. But he informed me that I should not be deceived by his misleading outward appearance. He was convinced that serious pathology was lurking in his body, with diagnoses yet to be determined. He told me he had become disenchanted with his local physician in a neighboring state, so he had driven all that way to see me. I later learned he picked our hospital at random, and I was called because I was on the schedule that night for unattached patients. That was just one of many untruths Michael would dispense before he was through with me.

Michael's primary complaint was reported as high fever. Even though his temperature was normal for three hours in the E.R., he insisted it had been routinely as high as 104 over the last several weeks. Once he arrived in his room his temperature did become elevated. It was so high that I consulted an infectious disease specialist to help with the case. Still, no definite source of infection could be found, and when his temperature was taken with the ear thermometer, it quickly returned to normal. Nevertheless, we felt compelled to continue evaluating Michael's condition. Cultures were taken from virtually every bodily fluid, and multiple X rays were performed. Still no illness was found. It was a remarkably confounding case.

The next morning I presented Michael with the results of the tests thus far. He seemed very concerned that we couldn't establish a diagnosis, but he was hardly surprised. He seemed to be enjoying the procession of medical professionals coming in and out of his room. Before I could leave him that morning, he snapped his finger as he remembered one more thing he wanted to share with me. It had to do with the chest pains he had been having. He said he had forgotten to mention them until that second.

During the next few hours, we performed EKGs, cardiac enzymes, and various imaging studies, but still we found no abnormality. The cardiologist assured and reassured Michael that his heart was quite healthy, but Michael seemed skeptical about our test results.

"Yeah, they told my uncle Raymond that very same thing. He dropped dead the next day with a massive coronary. Never can be too careful you know," Michael told him.

The cardiologist ordered another twenty-four hours of heart monitoring and another two sets of enzymes. He then called to let me know Michael would be with us at least another day.

"Never can be too careful, you know," he told me.

The next morning, as if by magic, Michael reported that the chest pains were totally gone. But his recovery was short-lived. Only moments after I left his room, Michael summoned a nurse to evaluate him for severe dizziness and sweating. He appeared to be in great distress, but he had the presence of mind to suggest that a blood sugar test might be in order.

"I've had a few spells of hypoglycemia in the past," he told her. "It might be my low blood sugar acting up again."

The nurse called me with the result, and it was indeed low. She seemed truly concerned about his fragile condition and wanted to know what we could do to stabilize him. I must admit, I was growing tired of his games. I immediately decided I no longer wanted to be a part of the charade, so I asked the nurse to draw some more blood and send it to the lab. Michael was informed that I would come back by that afternoon to discuss the results with him. She said he sat there with a pitiful look on his face, sipping orange juice while the blood was drawn. But I was confident. I knew I had him.

When I returned to see him later that day, I was armed with all the information I needed to expose him. I told Michael I knew why his fever had been up, why he had the chest pains, and why his blood sugar was low. And I solved the great mystery in only one day.

"That's fantastic, Doctor. I knew you could help me. Please tell me exactly what's wrong with me."

Believe me, I was happy to do that.

"Well, Michael, physically, there isn't anything wrong with you. But mentally, there appears to be a significant problem. For whatever reasons, I believe you have been manipulating our oral thermometers to give the appearance of fever. That's why it was always normal when checked in your ear. You haven't figured out a way to trick that instrument yet. As for the chest pains, I believe they were totally manufactured as well."

Michael stated, "Well, Doctor, I really can't believe you would say such things to me."

"Oh, keep listening," I told him. "It gets much better."

"Your big mistake was this morning when you had the hypoglycemic event. You see, Michael, when I sent your blood to the lab, I had it tested for medication that might have been taken to purposely lower your glucose reading. Would you like to guess what this test revealed?"

He turned his head to the window and mumbled a faint "no."

But since he had driven all that way and since it was really no trouble at all, I decided to show him the result anyway. The medication *was* present in his blood sample, proving he had caused the spell intentionally to get our attention.

"Now that this is all out in the open, there really is something I can do to help you. It will involve a transfer to the psychiatric unit for counseling and possibly even medication. I know that's probably not what you wanted to hear, but I really think this could help you. It's the only way you can have any hope of getting over your problem."

Michael declined my suggestion for psychiatric help. He went on to tell me he had seen psychiatrists before, bunches of them, and he was convinced that most of them were crazier than he was. (Then he gave some other arguments that were not quite as difficult to refute.) Finally, though, he said he would like to think it over for a few days and get back to me. I never saw or heard from him again. He packed his bag, left the hospital, and moved on down the road to present his rare collection of complaints to his next physician.

I thought about Michael a few weeks later as I was doing some of the final paperwork on his hospital chart. Even though none of us like to have the wool pulled over our eyes, I was happy that I had eventually solved his puzzle. Since that time I have realized there are a couple of things about this job that truly get under my skin. One is being faced with an ill patient who, despite all my best efforts, cannot seem to improve. We as physicians recognize this as part of the natural progression of life, but it is a difficult thing to accept. What is even more difficult to accept, however, is the occasional patient who *could*, but for whatever reason *will* not, get better.

I have come to believe the best response to such a case is to remind myself that some patients will never embrace the healing advice I have for them. Some are going to choose to live their lives without accepting the cure. Some people find it is easier to coast through life clinging to illness and coaxing sympathy than expending the energy necessary to make themselves better. The patients who *will* accept help are rewarding to work with. As for the rest, I put them out of my thoughts, and I move on down the road to the next patient who wants to get better. It was something I learned years ago from a professor in medical school. I don't think I'll ever forget what he told me.

"The most important determinant in many patients' recovery is their decision as to whether or not they actually want to get well," he said. "Always remember, if they don't want to improve their situation, you will never be able to make them. You cannot force people to do what's in their best interest."

His words have been valuable in my medical practice. And they have helped me sleep a lot better at night knowing that once I've given patients the best advice I have, there is little more I can do. After all, I can do only so much. Ultimately, people have to make some important decisions in life for themselves.

Chapter 19

THE PERFECT GIFT

It was still dark, but I could see the light frost on the ground that morning as I made my way to the hospital. It was the week before Christmas, and decorations were everywhere. Even in the hospital there were constant reminders of the season. Each nurse's station had its own tree decorated appropriately with tongue depressors, syringes, and other makeshift ornaments. It was an attempt to ease the difficulty for the people unfortunate enough to be sick during the holidays.

I pulled into the doctors' parking lot as usual, but it was not my usual trip to make rounds. The security guard gave a second look since he wasn't accustomed to seeing me in jeans, then waved me through. I told him I was there today only as a visitor, going to see a surgical patient. I had planned to take the day off for weeks. After all, my dad was having cataract surgery, and I wanted to be there.

He denied it, but I knew he was a little apprehensive, so I went to provide reassurance. I remembered at least a couple of times when he had done the same for me.

I visited with the surgeon, an old friend of mine, and listened as he explained the operation fully to my parents. I realized as he was talking that there is no such thing as a routine procedure when it is to be done on your family member. Risks were mentioned, possible complications explained, consent forms signed. Everything was in order. Mom kissed Dad, then said good-bye as they rolled him away to the surgical suite. He was understandably nervous but eager to proceed. He had grown intolerant of the progressive clouding of his vision in his left eye. It was especially frustrating for one with a history of seeing everything so distinctly.

I have discovered that describing my dad adequately is difficult. His work as a preacher, minister, and educator has spanned well over fifty years. He has long been a source of strength and encouragement, not only to my family, but also to countless others. The best I can do in my description is to refer you to 1 Corinthians 13. As you read, you will see him. He "suffers long" (especially while I was growing up). He is kind. He does not envy. He has always rejoiced in the truth. He bears all things, believes all, hopes all, endures all. He has never failed me. He is the most Christlike person I have ever known. He would be embarrassed by that comment, but it is nonetheless true.

So I went to wait, to visit, to give support. I thought Mom might enjoy the company. Besides, I knew Dad would be more than a handful after surgery. He would want to speed up his recovery, prematurely take off the eye patch, skip his medicine. He may be a good dad, but he is not a good patient. I knew she would need some assistance.

I sat with her in the waiting room while the procedure was being done. We talked, we laughed, and I was faced with a bit of irony. I was forced to sit there with nothing to read but terribly outdated magazines. Mom and I discussed our amazement that Dad has, at the age of sixty-five, reentered the classroom and finished his classwork at Auburn University. He will soon be receiving his Ph.D. in English education. When asked recently by a fellow student why at his age he had returned to school, he thought about it, then replied that he had decided it would look good in his obituary.

During that time in the waiting room, I thought about the unpleasant nature of cataracts. They progressively darken the view of the world, robbing their victims of their vision, heartlessly stealing their gift of sight. So bad are they that it is often a life-changing experience to have the little thieves removed. Patients are often overwhelmed by the difference. They are once again blessed with clear vision. They view with ease things that were once dark.

Soon the surgeon arrived and told us that the surgery was a little more complicated than expected, the cataract a little thicker than anticipated. He described it as stubborn. *Good choice of words*, I thought. The good news was that it had been a success. The new lens was implanted, and everything had gone well.

I watched as they rolled Dad into recovery with a patch on his eye, a hairdo that would have made Don King jealous, and a flimsy hospital gown that revealed a little more than it should have. But he was okay, and we were relieved. He looked slightly sedated, but I knew things were back to normal when he tugged at the sleeve of his nurse and asked if he could have something to eat. By then he had been fasting for about sixteen hours, his normal limit being no more than three. Any longer than that without food, and he has been known to declare a state of famine, go stand in the front yard, and await rescue planes from the Red Cross. Fortunately his breakfast soon arrived, and all was well.

The next couple of days consisted mostly of

couch time for him. There was some pain, some swelling around the eye, but overall he was extremely pleased. He had already begun to notice a significant improvement in his vision. Even though he wasn't 100 percent, it was nice having the family together for Christmas. We talked about old times. We told stories by the fire and relaxed in each other's company.

I remembered how similar it was to Christmas while I was growing up. My parents were very good to us, always giving us everything we needed and most of what we wanted. My wish list usually included the newest electronic gadget, usually some sports items, various games and toys. But I was always curious why, in addition to those necessities, I would also get socks, sweaters, and a coat. I didn't want them, I hadn't asked for them, and I certainly didn't need them. I was convinced that any money wasted on clothes could have been much better spent in the toy department. But as the weeks passed, batteries went dead, game pieces were lost, and the latest in electronic tech-nology short-circuited, leaving most of the Christmas haul dysfunctional. Without fail, I even-tually dug through my closet on a cold winter morning looking for that unappreciated sweater or searching for those discarded socks.

It wasn't until later in life that I realized that my

parents had known what I needed all along. I guess there are some things you can't see until you get a little older. Some levels of maturity come only with time. I knew it would be the same with my kids as well.

A few days later I sat by the tree and watched my children as they frantically opened their Christmas presents. There were the usual toys and games, but there were also a few sweaters, a couple of coats, and even, heaven forbid, a few pairs of socks. Of course, they were quickly tossed aside in the excitement of the moment, but I chuckled, knowing they would resurface some cold winter morning.

I must admit I enjoyed the holidays more than usual that year since the family had the opportunity to be together and since Dad was doing well. And I was reminded that Christmas of something else, a wonderful present that was given long ago. I rummaged through my spiritual closet to find the greatest gift of all, and once again I was extremely thankful that our Father knew what was best. I was thankful that despite all the superficial things I might ask for, He knew exactly what I needed all along.

Chapter 20

PAID IN FULL

I felt a sense of sadness as I realized for the first time that the voice on the phone was trembling and unsteady. I remembered another time, years before, when that voice was strong and forceful. The years, however, had taken their toll on Granddad, and his age was beginning to catch up with him.

As we talked, he reluctantly told me that he had been sick for a while, suffering with sharp pains in his abdomen. He called because he wondered if there was anything I might be able to do to help him. He said the last couple of weeks had been a pretty difficult time for him. The discomfort was growing steadily worse. Initially, it started with mild nausea, but right-upper-quadrant abdominal pain soon followed. Finally, he lost his appetite, and anything he did eat amplified the agony. He was beginning to feel fatigued, slightly feverish, and very weak.

I asked why he hadn't called sooner. He said he knew how busy I was, and he hated to bother me. That from the man who took me to the first baseball game I ever saw.

Since he lived more than a hundred miles away, it took a bit of doing, but my parents had him in my office bright and early the next morning. He was a little embarrassed by all the attention, but he came, willing at least to humor me. That day I also realized his thinking was not as clear as it had always been. The early stages of Alzheimer's disease were beginning to show.

This illness we call Alzheimer's disease is a terrible thing, robbing older people of their memory, their concentration and, eventually, even their dignity. It is indeed a progressive, painful, and insidious killer.

I did my best to reassure Granddad that everything would be fine as we admitted him to the hospital for a thorough battery of tests. I gave him a few final words of instruction, then stood to shake his hand, man to man. But before I could, he pressed his head against my chest as he hugged me, and he thanked me for taking care of him. I learned that day that there's a point in life when you stop worrying so much about appearances and start showing people how you really feel. I wasn't there just yet, but Granddad had been for some time. I put down his chart, hugged him back, and told him I'd be around to check on him in a few hours.

During the hospital evaluation, I watched my mom pamper and care for him much the way she had done for me when I was a child. Her behavior angered me slightly, and I wanted to scold her for being so overprotective of him, but deep inside I knew it was necessary. I was saddened to think that the once strong man now required such close care and supervision, especially since I knew he would need more of both in the years to come.

That night Mom and I accompanied him to the radiology department where an ultrasound of his abdomen was performed. It revealed, as I had expected, a diseased gallbladder full of stones. I immediately called one of my surgeon friends, and the time for the operation was set. Because of Granddad's age, extra precaution would be taken to assure that the procedure would be free of complications. Granddad was ready, even eager, to proceed since the pain was almost unbearable.

The surgery took place the following morning, and Granddad came through with flying colors. His postoperative course, however, was more eventful. The lingering effects of the anesthesia, compounded by his being in a strange place, confused Granddad. That night he became totally disoriented and began having flashbacks to base-ball games he had played in more than sixty years ago. He was agitated and even combative for a while. Finally, with some calm reassurance (and a couple of vials of IV Valium), we managed to calm him down a bit.

Later that evening with Granddad finally fast asleep, I left the hospital so I, too, could get some rest. Unfortunately, the man in the next bed was equally confused. After several minutes of scream-ing loudly, he managed to wake Granddad and per-suade him to help him out of his restraints. Granddad, not realizing the restraints had been placed to protect the man, took his pocketknife and cut his roommate free. Then, showing the compassion of a true good Samaritan, Granddad continued his good deed by personally escorting the man to the elevator and assisting him to the hospital lobby. It was an all-out jailbreak. Their escape was almost complete when, totally by chance, they were spotted and detained by hospi-tal security for questioning.

The next morning Granddad remembered none of the events. He was simply upset because his knife was missing. I didn't have the heart to tell him it had been confiscated as exhibit A by the security staff.

The entire incident was soon forgotten, and

within a few days Granddad was as good as new, ready to leave the hospital. He was beginning to think more clearly, but another giant wave of confusion was about to come ashore. It happened when we stopped at the business office to sign some papers and take care of his bill.

Granddad knew he was covered by Medicare, which took care of most of the charges. *That* much he remembered. What he did not know was that the hospital had agreed to waive any outstanding balance as a courtesy to me. That part really perplexed him. Even after I made several attempts to explain it to him, Granddad still could not understand what was taking place. He was sure some sinister plot was under way to take advantage of him. I could do little but smile as he told the accounting people he had never seen a hospital that didn't expect payment of some kind. He went on to tell them he wasn't sure they knew what they were talking about. He told them they had better check their figures again. "And by the way," he said, "while I was here somebody stole my knife. You can check on that, too, while you're at it!" He couldn't comprehend how he could incur such a debt, only to have it canceled.

It was a memorable scene. I still remember the frustrated, yet determined, look on the face of the clerk as she explained to Granddad for the third time: "Sir, the charges have been taken care of 100 percent. You can go now. Your bill has been paid in full!" Finally, with great hesitation, he appeared to accept her explanation. Moments later as we were leaving the hospital, he looked over at me, winked, and reminded me to let him know when he needed to make a payment. I smiled again, put my arm around him, and assured him I would do that.

Driving home, I glanced over at his aging face and was again saddened as I realized his moments of confusion would continue. I knew eventually they would worsen to the point that he could no longer care for himself. I looked at him that day in a new light. Before long, he would be leaving us behind. It was a hard pill to swallow, to think I would soon have to say good-bye to the gentle gray-haired fellow who had been such an influence on my life.

Still, as I looked at him, I found consolation in one thought. I knew when that day occurred, Granddad would be ready to go because he had lived the kind of life that he wanted, full of love for God and his family. And I realized that when he finally leaves this earth, there will be no more confusion for him. When he stands before the counter of eternity, he will be happy to hear the explanation he has been expecting for a long time.

I know he will understand fully when he hears the wonderful words: "Your charges have been taken care of 100 percent. You can go on in now. Your bill has been paid in full."

Chapter 21

PROCRASTINATION'S PRICE

Caroline had worked as a respiratory therapist for the last fifteen years. I had seen her as a patient only periodically for routine things: respiratory infections, an occasional bladder infection, nothing out of the ordinary. Nothing, that is, until today. She was almost frantic as I entered the room, so I didn't take time for the usual pleasantries. Her speech was rapid, her voice high-pitched, as she began to explain how she found it.

"Routine monthly check," she said, and there it was. At first she thought she imagined it, so she checked again, then her husband checked, but there was no mistake. It was definitely there. Caroline experienced the worst nightmare of many a female patient; she found a lump in her breast. It was a discovery that would change her life forever.

I stepped outside the room and waited as the

nurse helped Caroline into a gown. A phone call detoured me for a few minutes, and when I returned, I could sense her impatience. During the exam, I tried to show no emotion, but I confirmed that she was correct. There was a lump, and it was a significant abnormality. In my mind it was cancer, at least until proved otherwise. Before I finished examining her, I began to outline the necessary workup in my mind. After some questioning I learned that, despite the fact that Caroline was forty-eight years old, she had never had a mammogram.

"Never really felt the need," she said. "No history of breast cancer in my family. Mom lived to be ninety-one years old."

I wasn't sure if that was intended to make her or me feel better, but it did neither.

"Caroline, we need to set you up for a mammogram immediately to get a better look at this," I said. I was optimistic that I hadn't felt any lymph node enlargement or other mass. I hoped that if it was cancer, we were catching it at an early stage. "Even if the mammogram doesn't show anything, we'll still need to get a surgeon to evaluate you," I told her. I explained that the risks were too great to take the situation lightly.

She nodded in total agreement, and we proceeded with our plan as rapidly as possible. The mammogram was done that afternoon. After its completion, Caroline called the office almost hourly, checking to see if the report was back. I assured her I would call as soon as it came. Eventually, it did, and it was not encouraging at all. A 1.5 centimeter mass was identified in the area where we had felt the lump. It was "ominous in appearance," according to the radiologist, and contained numerous microcalcifications, often seen with malignancy. In other words, it was cancer until proved otherwise. Caroline had come to the office to get the results personally, so we sat together as I explained exactly what we knew thus far. She wept as I told her.

The biopsy was to be done the following day. She was understandably nervous, but she said she was anxious to proceed. She wanted to have an answer. She wanted to get it over with. As she left my office, I silently hoped for the best and prepared for the worst.

I saw patients as usual the next afternoon, but in the back of my mind I remembered Caroline. I was waiting for the phone call from the surgeon with the preliminary biopsy report. Finally, he called, but not with the message I was expecting. He called to say that she hadn't shown.

"She didn't keep her appointment. Do you want me to call her?" he asked. I assured him that wouldn't be necessary, and I told him we would take care of it from our office. I hung up the phone, totally convinced there was some logical explanation for what had happened. I couldn't have been more wrong.

"I changed my mind," Caroline said. She had a change of heart and decided she wanted to think about it for a couple of days, maybe longer. I reinforced the need to proceed as soon as possible. I suggested she might want a second or third opinion if necessary, but it was no use. Caroline was paralyzed by her fear. She was too afraid to have the biopsy done—afraid it might really be cancer, afraid of the possibility of losing her breast, afraid of dying.

I called her several times over the next few weeks, asking her to reconsider. I even sent a certified letter, but to no avail. She was always grateful for the call. She said she appreciated my concern, but she just wasn't ready yet. She said she would let me know if she changed her mind again, but that never happened. The weeks quickly became months, and Caroline was lost to follow-up for more than a year.

I still remember the frantic look on the nurse's face when she told me, "Caroline's husband is on the phone. Will you talk to him?" It had been thirteen months since her last visit. They were visiting family members in another state when Caroline developed constant chest pain and shortness of breath. They drove back into town that night and were in my office early the next morning.

Caroline didn't look well at all. She had lost a lot of weight, her gait was unsteady, and she was noticeably pale. A blood count showed her to be severely anemic, and a breast exam revealed a much larger mass. She was admitted to the hospital immediately. Biopsies were done and, as we had feared, were positive for malignancy. CT scans demonstrated metastatic disease involving her spine, pelvis, and both lungs. She wept again as I told her the results.

Caroline had worked in the hospital for a long time, and she had taken care of countless cancer patients. She knew all too well what was to come. Surgery would be of little or no benefit. Even chemotherapy would most likely have no effect. The disease was too far advanced. I didn't want to take away all hope, but there really wasn't much to offer her.

Over the next forty-eight hours Caroline deteriorated rapidly. Pain medicine was required to keep her comfortable, and oxygen, too, was needed to assist her failing lungs. We were quickly losing the battle. After talking with her family, I asked her children to leave the room so I could have the conversation with Caroline that I had been dreading. I had hoped it could be postponed a while, but as I witnessed the rapid progression of her illness, I knew it could wait no longer. With her husband present, I spoke to her openly and honestly.

"Caroline, I don't know if you've thought about this, but you have some very important decisions to make." The look in her eyes revealed that she was way ahead of me. She knew her respiratory system was failing rapidly due to the tumor. She would not be able to breathe much longer without assistance. I could tell that she had already made her decision, but I listened intently. She pulled off her oxygen mask, motioned for me to come closer, and said emphatically, "No respirator!" She wanted to be sure that she was not misunderstood.

After more discussion, her husband was in agreement, and her wishes were honored. Two days later I stood by her side in the intensive care unit as she died, her left hand in mine, her right hand in her husband's. That time the tears were mine.

After arrangements had been made, I dictated the record, signed off the chart, and left the hospital. I had tried to separate myself from the case emotionally, but I had failed. That one I had felt personally. That one had hurt.

I thought how tragic it was that Caroline didn't agree to treatment a year ago. How sad it was to be so close to a lifesaving cure, only to reject it through refusal or procrastination and ultimately lose something of such great value. But nothing could minimize the pain for the grieving family. Nothing could reverse the terrible loss I had just witnessed. Nothing could undo what was done. It was too late. Caroline made her choice long ago. Still, I knew, even as I stood by her side in those final moments, that she would have paid any price to have the opportunity to make the decision again. The all-important decision that proved to be so expensive. The decision that cost Caroline everything.

Chapter 22

THE MIDNIGHT HOUR

Deb and I had planned for several weeks to have an actual date. The arrangements, however, had not exactly been easy to make. We had to work around my erratic schedule and try to locate a baby-sitter who could be ready at a moment's notice. Fortunately, it all fell into place. At the last minute our preacher and his wife, our good friends Gary and Leisa Bradley, were able to keep Lindsay.

It was the spring of 1990, and our baby was almost a year old. Even though we knew she was in good hands, we left reluctantly. We may have been a little overly cautious, but hey, we were new parents; it was expected of us. We went out for a nice dinner, took in a movie, and remarked on how we should have a date more often. Nevertheless, I was concerned about permanent wrist damage from looking at my watch so often, so we raced back and picked up our little girl. It was an easy diagnosis to make: acute baby withdrawal syndrome (common in first-time parents).

We sat and chatted briefly, thanked our sitters, then packed up all of our age-appropriate learning toys and prepared to leave. But as I made my way to the door, Gary stopped me. "Oh, by the way, Doc, I wanted you to look at something for me before you go." He reached for his forehead, parted his hair, and revealed a two-centimeter oval skin lesion on his left front scalp. It was red, swollen, and inflamed. It looked infected. *This will need to be drained,* I thought, and I mentally began juggling my schedule to work him in as soon as possible.

"How long has this been there?" I asked, more to make conversation than anything else.

Gary paused, thought for a minute, then said, "Oh, about two or three years, I guess. I'm not exactly sure."

At that moment I feared we might have a problem, potentially a serious one. Due to the size of the lesion I decided I would send him to a dermatologist to get another opinion. I arranged the referral the very next day.

A biopsy was done immediately, which revealed that it was indeed a cancer. It was a rare dermatofibrosarcoma, an aggressive, locally invasive, potentially lethal cancer.

Stunned and confused, Gary brought the pathology report to my office and sat with me, looking for answers, searching for reassurance. I could give neither. Even the textbooks were of little help regarding the uncommon, unwelcome invader. The only thing I knew for sure was that it had to be removed, and the sooner, the better.

After consulting with the dermatologist, I referred Gary to a local plastic surgeon, and the time for the operation was set. We were all nervous, but we knew we had to proceed. Within a week the surgery was done, and Gary tolerated it without any complication. Gary and Leisa sat in the hospital room, waiting anxiously for the pathology report. That evening they learned the outcome of the operation. Gary got the report he had most feared.

"It's spread farther than I had anticipated," his surgeon said. "I'm afraid we'll have to go back and try again. If, however, it has spread past the skull and into the brain, the surgery will be much more difficult. I must warn you, if that's the case, it could even be fatal."

Gary and Leisa felt their entire world crumble with those few words. Cancer? Potentially fatal? At the age of thirty-two? Was there some mistake? Oh, there were plenty of questions, but there were precious few answers.

The next several days were very difficult for the two of them and their three young boys. Recovery time was needed, time for Gary to regain his strength from one operation and prepare for another. All the while the nagging doubt began to build, and questions of "Why me?" pounded in his brain. He began to wonder, after years of being a counselor, after years of giving advice to trust in God, after speaking at numerous seminars, Would his faith sustain him? Would his hope carry him? And, he told me, he began to wonder, Would his God save him? The doubt would not subside.

Leisa decided to call the school to inform the boys' teachers of the situation and their special needs. After lengthy discussions with the first two teachers, she dialed the third. It was the teacher of their middle son, their eight-year-old, William. She began the emotionally draining story once again, but the teacher interrupted.

"Oh, Mrs. Bradley, you don't need to say more. You see, Will has told me all about it."

That very day, as she had dismissed the class for recess, Will had stayed behind, alone. With the other children gone and the room silent, he reached under his desk and pulled out his Bible. He quietly approached the teacher's desk and announced with the soft voice of an innocent child: "Ma'am, my dad has cancer." There was a long pause as she looked up to see Will standing before her. Then with a tear trickling down his cheek, he summoned the courage to ask, "Would it be okay if I read my Bible to you, if I read you a story about how Jesus died for me?"

Gary had often told him, "Son, they may not be allowed to read it to you, but you can sure read it to them." It seems that Will, too, was suffering from the stressful ordeal. He was feeling his own very real and very personal pain. Even at his young age, he knew that no intellectual source held the keys to finding comfort. He knew no certified therapist could provide the solace he needed. No, Will acted with wisdom far beyond his years. He gathered his pain. He collected his doubts and his fears. He packaged them neatly and carefully, and took them to the only place he knew he could find strength. He took them to the Cross.

In a hospital bed across town, his father was in the process of learning that same lesson. Gary was approaching his own personal midnight, and though he didn't want to be there alone, he didn't yet seem to know where to turn. In fact, he tried his best to hide his pain, and he thought he covered it quite well.

"How ya doin', Gary?"

"Oh, just fine," he would say.

"Feelin' okay today?"

"Great!" he would answer.

"Anything we can do?"

"No, got it all taken care of. Thanks anyway."

The facade seemed impenetrable, or so he thought.

But his charade did not fool everyone. Just before the time to return to the operating room for the second surgery, Gary was visited by a close and very dear friend.

"How are ya, buddy?" the friend asked.

"I'm fine," came the well-rehearsed reply. But this time it just didn't float.

His friend confronted him. "That may be what you tell everyone else, but I don't want to hear it. I want to hear the truth."

For the first time since the diagnosis of his cancer had been made, Gary faced his fear and was honest with himself. He put aside the false veil of confidence, broke into tears, and confessed that he was scared. He was frightened beyond belief, to the point that he didn't know if he could stand it anymore. He had always been so brave, a source of strength, a rock. Now, however, he wondered if there was such a thing as real strength. He felt very afraid and very alone. His good friend embraced him, then they prayed together.

Moments later Gary was rolled down the sterile corridor and into the cold surgical suite, his fate still unknown. After several hours of surgery, Gary was returned to his room and the companionship of his wife and friends. That afternoon seemed like an eternity. There was nothing more to do but wait, hope, and pray.

Later that evening he heard the words he will never forget. "Gary, we got it all!" proclaimed a delighted surgeon. There were more prayers, that time prayers of thanksgiving, and there were also tears of joy. At the hands of a skillful surgeon, Gary's life had been spared. He had been given a second chance.

But as he would soon learn, the hard times were far from over. Six more surgeries would be needed to reconstruct the tennis-ball-sized crater where the cancer had once resided. Each one was marked by its unique pain, its unique problems. Sometimes there was bleeding, sometimes infection. Yet all were necessary to rebuild the scalp. Though intellectually Gary knew that, the mental anguish mounted.

Gary did a lot of soul-searching during that time. Even though the cancer demons had been chased away for the present, uncertainty was always lingering around the corner. There was a good chance the cancer might recur. There was the possibility that more reconstructive procedures might be needed as the tissue settled into place. Every possible negative scenario found its way into Gary's mind. He had no shortage of pessimistic thoughts. He tried to ignore them, yet he couldn't seem to clear them from his head. It was only then, Gary admits, that he found the peace he had been looking for. It was then that he took a cue from his son Will, and found the strength to turn the whole thing over to his Lord.

Gary admits he is a much better person for having endured his health problems, but it would have been hard to believe that at the time. Now, however, after several years of celebrating his victory over cancer, it's much easier to put into perspective. At times it can be difficult for him to talk about, but he insists on doing it anyway. It's for his benefit, of course, but also for the benefit of countless others. Gary now travels the country to tell his story to people who are in pain. He has entitled his testimonial "When Midnight Approaches," so named after a poem he was once given. He shares the poem by an anonymous author with all who will listen:

Every man has his midnight. That time when feeble eyes can't penetrate the darkness. When the oil of our Christian lamp is low, or maybe life has almost snuffed it out. Midnight. When we find ourselves chained, bound, and beaten. When death itself would be a welcome visitor. The lasting beauty of Christianity is not witnessed in lives that have been sheltered from the storms and untouched by the world. . . . If we would comprehend the real weight, beauty and worth of Christianity, then we must view it at the midnight hour.

Gary always reads that poem as he concludes his story, a story that is much easier for him to tell now that I can assure him that he is completely healthy. And all of us who know him are grateful for his good health. Grateful that the life of such a good man, a good husband, a good father, a good minister, was spared. Grateful that he tells his story and that he graciously allowed me to share it with you.

I had lunch with Gary recently, and we talked for a while about his cancer, about his doubts, about his surrender to the Lord. We talked about the fact that although he had beaten the illness, there will someday be another. Eventually, it's a path we must all travel.

Before we parted that day, he told me one final thing. He shook my hand and said, "I don't know when I'll leave this world, none of us can know that, but if you're there with me when I do, please hold my hand. Please tell me that you love me, and remind me that God loves me. Because I now know without a doubt that it's true, and He's the only One I trust, the only One I need beside me as midnight approaches."

Chapter 23

THE RUNAWAY

Kim had been under a tremendous amount of stress lately. At least, that was the story she told me as we talked in my office for the first time. I had no real reason to be suspicious. She was the well-groomed, well-dressed daughter of a respected local businessman. She had even brought along her two children, and they, too, seemed concerned as their mother related the story of her recent painful divorce.

In retrospect I realized that she never even asked me for the Valium. I offered it to her. After all, it was considered appropriate in such a situation, at least for short-term use. She seemed sincerely grateful for my concern, and she agreed to give the sedatives a chance to work to see if they would reduce her anxiety. She took the prescription, thanked me, and left the office, agreeing to return in two weeks for a follow-up appointment.

She seemed to be such a nice young woman, but

I was soon to learn differently. I had no idea of the impact she would have on the way I practiced medicine. There was simply no clue to warn me of the adventure that lay in store.

The next day our office received a call from Kim, apologizing for being such a bother, stating that she had somehow managed to misplace her prescription. She asked if we could simply phone in a replacement for her. Normally, that would arouse suspicion, but she seemed above such misdoing. After all, she was from such a good family and had such sweet children. I was slightly embarrassed for even questioning her in my mind. "Of course, refill it," I said.

Two days later another call came. Kim frantically reported that her car had been stolen, containing her purse and all of her medication. *How unfortunate*, I thought to myself. At that point I didn't care who she was or how well she was dressed. I could no longer deny my suspicion.

"Perhaps you would like to come back in to discuss this with the doctor?" my nurse asked. Kim promptly produced several reasons why that would be quite impossible and politely declined, requesting yet more medication. I mustered some politeness and refused to give her the refill. Her attitude quickly changed. Kim became very rude, verbally abusive, and angrily hung up the phone. I thought maybe, just maybe, that would be the last I heard from her, but I was mistaken.

Later that day I received phone calls from three local pharmacies, each asking for confirmation on prescriptions for Kim. All had been phoned in by "my nurse." All of the appropriate license numbers had been given; all the details were exactly correct. Most were for controlled substances: Valium, pain pills, various narcotics, even one for birth control pills.

I was angry about the incident. I was also slightly embarrassed that I had been duped. After overcoming the initial humiliation, I decided I would not go down without a fight. I spent most of the next hour on the phone with local, state, and federal authorities giving them all the details I could remember. They were extremely helpful, but said there was little they could do unless they were able to catch her in the act. I soon found out, however, that would not be easy. No, Kim was smart. Heavily sedated, maybe, but smart. She was no rookie at the game. I constantly tried to devise a plan to trap her, yet all the while the phone calls kept coming in.

Every day at least two pharmacists called to question a large quantity of narcotics on a phoned-in prescription. Each was called in by a woman claiming to be my nurse. Each one was for Kim.

Each one bumped my blood pressure up another five points. I wondered how many other calls there were, prescriptions that were filled without even so much as a question. It had become personally embarrassing to me and quite unnerving.

Finally, after weeks of my feeling powerless to stop her, she made her mistake. I was busy with patients one Friday afternoon when I was interrupted by a call from a pharmacist in another state. He was questioning an unusually large order for Valium. I knew immediately it was her; it had to be. I called the local police who, incidentally, were all too familiar with Kim. They left to pick her up, but she had become suspicious because of the long delay and had fled the scene. The search for Kim was on.

After several hours the police were able to locate her. She was hiding at a friend's apartment, barricaded in the bedroom. She had locked herself in, refusing to open the door for anyone, including her friend. The phone was off the hook; the blinds were closed; all the lights were out. She was just sitting there in the dark. When the police finally reached her, she offered no excuses. She just collapsed on the floor and cried. The game and the running were finally over. They called to let me know she was in custody, yet even in my anger I couldn't help feeling pity for her. After all, she was a sick young woman, desperately in need of guidance and counseling.

I later learned from her family that it had been a recurring story since Kim was sixteen years old. Initially, it started with wild parties with her school friends, with alcohol and marijuana use. She was listed as a runaway twice before the age of eighteen, but each time she returned home. Each time she promised to straighten herself out, to give up the wild life and substance abuse. Each time, however, she did not keep her promises. She gradually made the transition from alcohol and street narcotics to prescription drugs. She learned they were much easier to obtain, much cheaper to buy, and much more socially acceptable.

Kim managed to dry out briefly during her early twenties, long enough to graduate from college with a degree in accounting, long enough to get married and have children. But then the running started again. Any little problem at work, any conflict at home, any trying situation at all, and Kim was off and running.

She had never been able to come to grips with who she really was; she couldn't identify her place in a productive society. So she ran. From one husband after another, from numerous jobs, from her parents, from her children, and from herself. She had turned to the narcotics as her escape. And though they had destroyed her life, the effects of the drugs had masked her pain—if only temporarily. When she sobered up and returned to reality, the pain returned. It was more than she could take, so off she ran to another bottle of pills, another town, another job, another man. She learned to outrun the police and evade her family, but the one thing that eluded her was to outrun herself. It was seemingly the only constant in her otherwise chaotic life.

I learned the details of Kim's tragic life in a long discussion with her father that weekend. After our talk I agreed not to press charges. He agreed to fund her rehabilitation. The courts agreed to oversee it with the warning that this would be her last chance. Next time there would be no mercy. Next time there would be prison.

I hoped she would be able to turn things around not only for herself, but also for her two boys. They were angry, confused, and forgotten. They were pawns in a game of deceit too complex for them to understand. Kim's first husband, the father of their children, also called me the following week. He called to ask for help and to thank me for not pressing charges.

"I know it probably sounds stupid," he told me, "but I guess I still love her. I know the boys do, too. They miss their mother so much when she's gone.

I know we didn't have very much when we were married, I mean, not much money or anything, but when we were together, we always seemed to be happy. I guess Kim just felt that she needed more. It just seemed that was never enough for her."

I hung up the phone feeling sorry for him. I was also glad I had not pursued having Kim charged with her crime. I felt strongly that I had done the right thing, knowing her only chance for survival was through a proper rehabilitation program. I thought a lot that day about her former husband. He was betrayed, rejected, repeatedly abandoned by Kim, yet he still wished things could be as they once were. He still wished she returned his love. I also thought about the faces of the two small boys I had seen with her that day in the office. The young fellows needed their mother and the stability of a loving family.

I didn't know exactly what Kim thought she might find out there. I wondered what high she needed to experience, what riches she needed to obtain, to make her view her life as a success. I wasn't even sure she knew what she wanted, but I hoped she would figure it out soon. I hoped eventually she would realize that the only thing of value, the most precious treasures she could ever hold, were right under her nose and had been all the time.

Chapter 24

FRED'S PROMISE

Ruby's face was pale and her silver hair was noticeably beginning to thin, but those were only a couple of the many signs that her health was rapidly failing. Sadly, the hospital bed she had occupied for the past two weeks was the only home she remembered. Her only contact with the past was a picture on her nightstand. The picture that reflected happier times was of Ruby and her devoted husband, Fred. The black-and-white picture must have been more than forty years old, but Fred brought it to help her remember. They were standing by a car outside an old cafe, arm in arm, just enjoying each other's company. And they were an attractive couple. It was sad to think that after all the years together Ruby couldn't even remember Fred's name. That was but one of the consequences of her progressive Alzheimer's disease.

I could tell the last couple of days had been

especially hard on Fred. Not only was he having to cope with losing his best friend of so many years, but he now seemed to be making an enemy. Ruby was confused and frightened most of the time, and in her deteriorating condition she became very mean and suspicious of her husband's actions. She accused him of "putting her in this place" so he could take all their money, get her out of the way, and "run off with one of those young girls that were in and out of there all the time."

I quietly motioned for Fred to step into the hall-way so I could speak with him privately. Besides the fact that we had some important issues to discuss, I knew he needed a few moments away from the tension in the room. I could tell he had reached his limit. I didn't know exactly how I would begin the discussion, but I knew I couldn't put it off any longer.

"I guess these last few days have been pretty hard on you, haven't they, Fred?"

"Yeah, Doc, they sure have. I don't see it gettin' any better, either, do you?"

"Well, that's what I wanted to speak with you about, Fred. You see, your wife's memory and her overall condition have gotten so bad that I really don't see how you'll be able to care for her at home. I think it may be time for you to consider letting us arrange some other place for her to live. Someplace where they're better equipped to deal with her special physical and emotional needs."

"You mean a nursing home, don't you, Doc?"

"Well, that's one option, Fred. And in all honesty, it's one I think you should seriously consider. Even if you were able to give her the care she needs at home, it would require every minute of your time. At your age, I'm afraid you wouldn't be able to keep up that pace for very long without compromising your own health."

When I made that last statement, Fred smiled and gave me a look of resignation. It seemed somewhat inappropriate at the time, but I would come to understand it much more fully in a few months.

Over the next several days the paperwork was completed, all the documentation was filed, and Ruby went to live in one of our local extended care facilities. On the day of her transfer, she was alert enough to realize what was happening. She reacted by punishing Fred one last time in my presence. Ruby told him she hated him for what he had done to her. She said she didn't know why she had ever married him in the first place, and she told him she never wanted to see him again. The accusations she had made a few days earlier resurfaced with the full force of her anger. Fred was accused of stealing her monthly check, of plotting her demise, of being unfaithful on numerous occasions. He looked at me in embarrassment, and with a small tear trickling down his right cheek, he reminded me she had not always been like that.

"I know, Fred, I know."

As we talked, Fred was gently wiping her forehead with a cool cloth. Despite the barrage of angry words, Fred's only thought was to comfort the woman he had loved so long. Soon Ruby became tired, and the harsh verbal attack stopped as she drifted off to sleep. Even with all her protests, Fred stood firm, and Ruby left for her new home.

The anger and the accusations, however, never let up. Still, Fred visited with his wife in the nursing home every day until death separated them.

I was on call that night in the E.R. when I saw Fred coming through the door. I asked him how Ruby was doing, and I saw a quick smile on his lips.

"A little better, Doc. She's doin' a little better. Thanks so much for taking such good care of her."

"But what about you, Fred? What brings you in to see us tonight?"

Fred looked as though he had lost at least thirty pounds since I saw him last. He was very pale, his skin was exceptionally dry, and he barely had enough strength to sit up on the stretcher. I sat down and reviewed his chart as the nurses drew some of his blood, took his temperature, and worked further to stabilize him. The chart had come from the office of a good friend, a well-known cancer specialist. I shook my head in disbelief as I reviewed the details of Fred's history. All that time taking care of his wife, and I never knew about Fred's colon cancer. The chart said he had surgery about a year ago, but the tumor had spread outside the wall of the colon before they could get to it. Usually, a course of chemotherapy would have been given, but I was puzzled to find no record of it. This entire situation seemed so strange. It was one that needed a little more explanation.

Another older fellow had accompanied Fred to the E.R. that night. His older brother had driven into town to be part of what little time Fred had left on this earth. I pulled the brother aside and asked him why Fred hadn't told anyone about his condition. Why hadn't he followed up with the oncologist? Why wasn't the chemotherapy given? Fred's brother told me that that was the way Fred wanted it.

"Oh, I tried to get him to have the treatments. I thought if there was any chance he might live even a few months longer, then we should at least give it a try. But Fred wouldn't go through with it. At first I thought he was just being stubborn, but then he explained it to me, and I understood. You see,

Fred knew that Ruby's health was going downhill fast. And he knew if he had those treatments, he would be very sick, very weak, and they could possibly even kill him.

"He knew he couldn't take care of Ruby in that condition, and he sure knew she wouldn't be able to take care of him. Besides, their funds were very limited, and he knew Ruby would need that money to live on. He didn't see any sense in spending it on expensive medicine for him when it wouldn't change the outcome of things. To tell you the truth, Doc, I think Fred was trying to hold out for the day when Ruby would go to the nursing home. He knew if he could take care of her for that long, his job would be done. Then she'd have people to take care of her, and he could leave her without feeling guilty. He would have done what he had always promised her he would do."

It was one of the most touching, most heart-warming stories of human compassion I had ever heard. I glanced through the glass separating me from Fred's exam room and knew I was looking at a very special individual. I saw a man who loved his wife enough to sacrifice his own life in order to take care of her, just as he had always said he would do. I knew that was a rare thing.

Fred died that night on the oncology floor of the hospital. He had long ago requested that no heroic measures be taken, so he went quietly and peacefully, the way he should have gone, the way he wanted to go. I was in the room not long after he was pronounced dead, and I had the opportunity to talk to Fred's brother one last time. He was standing by the window, crying softly and going through some of Fred's belongings.

Fred had packed a small suitcase before they left home. He had no way of knowing how long he might be staying at the time. I patted Fred's brother on the back and expressed my sympathy for his loss. I told him how much I admired his brother for taking such good care of his wife. I told him to let me know if there was any way I could help him. As he turned to thank me, I noticed a small object in his hand that he had taken from Fred's suitcase. It was a small black-and-white picture of a young, attractive couple. They were arm in arm, standing by a car in front of an old cafe. It was a picture of a sensitive, caring, wonderful man and the woman he loved more than anyone else on this earth. I looked one last time at the picture, and I realized something very valuable was lost that night. I realized the world had lost a hero.

Chapter 25

THE CARPENTER WITH THE CURE

Your blood count is dangerously low. I'm afraid we will have to operate again to have any chance of stopping the bleeding." Those were the words that Jeff heard from his surgeon in the fall of 1983. The reaction was near disbelief. The first surgery had been torture enough. Then the horribly irritating nasogastric tube had hung from his nose for the last three days. But to be forced to return for another operation? *Surely, this can't be happening,* Jeff thought. But it was.

Jeff had been admitted to the hospital earlier that week with a life-threatening hemorrhage from a perforated ulcer in his stomach. The corrective surgery had taken its toll on him, but he seemed to be turning the corner. He was still in the intensive care unit, yet each day had seen him grow stronger. The next day, if his improvement continued, he was scheduled to be transferred to a regular room. That's when he had the overwhelming sensation of nausea. Then the drainage from his suction tube turned an ominous crimson color. The bleeding had recurred. Jeff was faced with a second surgery, to try again to dam the flow of blood that seriously threatened to take his life.

The operation was a complete success. There would be no recurrent bleeding, but there was a price to be paid. Jeff had required rapid blood transfusions during that critical time. Six units in all had been given during the surgery. The blood had to be given, all of it, and given immediately. So, you see, there is really no way to know which one it was. But it was one of them. One of the small red bags that contained the lifesaving, oxygen-carrying red blood cells also harbored an evil villain. One of them was contaminated with the HIV virus. It would be two more years before adequate testing of our blood supply would be standard procedure. Two years full of political posturing and endless debate over such an important issue. Two years too late for Jeff.

I first met Jeff in 1993, ten years after the ill-fated transfusions. I saw a young, but very thin man lying before me in a hospital bed, once again struggling for his life. The torn shirt, dirty jeans, and stubbly facial hair revealed that his outward appearance had long taken a backseat to his struggle for survival. The enemy was Pneumocystis pneumonia, a common lung infection among people with AIDS. Jeff's chest X ray showed diffuse bilateral infiltrates, diagnostic for advanced pneumonia. To further complicate things, his cough was getting progressively worse, and his fever topped 103 degrees. Despite the constant IV and inhaled medications I had ordered, it looked as though Jeff might not make it. He had suffered other opportunistic infections over the years, but none so severe. Through it all, Jeff tried to keep a positive attitude, but he was beginning to realize that the end was near. After fighting so bravely for so long, he was growing tired of the battle.

That week I had several long talks with Jeff about AIDS, about social awareness, about people's conceptions and misconceptions of the disease. During the course of his illness, Jeff had learned some painful, yet eye-opening lessons about human nature. He had learned about people's fears: fear of the unknown, fear of being infected with the virus, fear of being around someone perceived as being different.

Since Jeff had never been married, many people incorrectly assumed that he was gay. "When they learned of my disease," Jeff told me, "they expressed sympathy, then gave me that look of . . . oh, well, I guess you got what you deserved." He duplicated the facial expression so precisely that I knew he had seen it quite often.

When he assured them he was not gay, they often pursued another line of questioning: "How long did you use IV drugs?" Or "Were you addicted to heroin, or were you just experimenting?" Again the looks were of pity, carefully mixed with righteous indignation and contempt.

"No drugs? Well, perhaps it was promiscuous heterosexual activity? Too many wild fraternity parties in college, huh?"

"No," came the answer again.

"I'm just so tired of their judgmental questioning. Tired of having people care more about the *way* I became infected than the fact that I'm struggling with this fatal disease. What people don't seem to realize," he told me, "is that no matter how I got AIDS, it's still the same disease. The infections are the same. The fatigue is the same. The pain is the same. I hate to say it, but I've gotten much more support from the people at the AIDS clinic than I have from most of the people I know at our church."

Jeff's experiences proved to be eye-opening for me as well. I was pleased I had gotten to know more about him from our talks and even more pleased that he recovered from that terrible case of pneumonia. Shortly after I released him from the hospital, however, Jeff began to develop dark lesions on his skin. He wondered when they would come. He knew exactly what they were, but he returned to see me for evaluation. He wanted to hear it from me.

He wandered into my office that afternoon looking quite depressed. He was sporting the same torn shirt, same stubbly beard, and baggy jeans that he pulled to midthigh as he showed me the lesions. It was an easy clinical diagnosis, yet I took a biopsy specimen for confirmation. The pathologist agreed; they were cancer. They were, as I had feared, diagnostic for Kaposi's sarcoma, cancerous skin lesions associated with AIDS. Their development, as Jeff well knew, was not a cause for optimism.

That same day, after having some blood drawn, Jeff went downtown to take part in his usual group counseling session. After the session, something unusual happened to him. Jeff and nine other members of the group, all AIDS patients, were standing outside the clinic. As they were discussing various medications and comparing skin lesions, they saw him, a rather common-looking person. He appeared to be a laborer of some sort, probably a construction worker judging by the calloused hands. The stranger approached them and began to talk. Apparently, he was so moved by their plight that he began to express great concern. After further discussion, he told them to go back inside and show themselves to the clinic director to have their conditions reevaluated.

As they went, something amazing happened. Jeff noticed that his skin lesions were gone. Not only that, he was shocked to realize that he was totally healed! Why, it was a miracle! *There is no cure for AIDS*, he thought to himself. Yet the evidence was incontrovertible. He was healed! They were all healed! The clinic director and all the infectious disease specialists were understandably astounded.

I know, that last part is a little hard to believe. And you know what, I'll bet it was hard for the folks in Galilee, too. I thought about Jeff's story recently when I read of our Lord's encounter with ten men who, like Jeff, were seriously ill. They had been diagnosed with leprosy—the AIDS of their day. Like Jeff, they were isolated, they were afraid, and they were without hope. With no antibiotics available, and with such a contagious disease, they had been forced to live outside the city, their only companions other people with leprosy. They were sentenced to endure a lonely, painful existence and eventually die without the closeness and support of loved ones.

Then they saw Him, their last glimmer of hope. He was rather common looking. He was just a simple carpenter. But they had heard the stories that many had been healed. Still they were unclean, their medical laws prevented them from even approaching Him, so they did the only thing they could. They begged Him for mercy.

And amazingly enough, I didn't read about any questions concerning how they had become infected. There was no evidence that background checks were done to see if they were the right kind of people to justify expending the energy necessary to perform a miracle.

As I said, I thought about Jeff recently, not long after he passed away. He was resting at home one afternoon when he became acutely short of breath and extremely weak. He managed to walk outside, but he couldn't get into the car. His brother ran over and caught him just as his breathing became shallow and irregular. He tried his best to wake him, but Jeff was totally unresponsive. His brother could do nothing more than hold him in his arms and watch as Jeff took his last breath. With tears in his eyes he brought Jeff's body through the automatic doors of the E.R., followed the nurse into an exam room, and waited there for the rest of the family. Most of the people in the waiting room drew back as Jeff's thin, pale, lifeless body was carried past them.

I arrived about an hour later. I remember seeing Jeff's mother standing in the corridor outside the E.R. They were not a wealthy family by any means. They were hardworking people, proud people. When she saw me, she forced a smile through her tears, walked over to me, and embraced me warmly. Her battle, too, was over. She was left with the unenviable task she had been dreading for a long time of having to bury her oldest son. Still, she thanked me for what I had done for Jeff, for listening to him, for respecting him. I told her I wished I could have done more to help him.

"Yes," she said, "and there are so many others. I just wish people understood what it's like to go through this. I wish they weren't so afraid to help."

I nodded in agreement and said the only thing that came to mind. "Someday," I told her. "Maybe someday."

Chapter 26

DECEPTIVE BEAUTY

I gripped the scalpel firmly and carefully shaved the crusty piece of skin from Kelly's arm. The lighter tones of the subcutaneous tissue were visible and provided a stark contrast to the darkly tanned exterior of her upper extremity. I glanced down at her chart and noticed she was only twenty-four years of age, yet the deep tan had gradually taken its toll on her. It had caused her to look years older.

After cleaning the wound with silver nitrate, I placed the unsightly fragment of flesh into a small plastic bottle and capped it tightly. The specimen labeled "abnormal skin lesion" left my office shortly thereafter and started its journey into the realm of the reference laboratory. The answer was in the hands of the pathologist.

I spoke honestly with Kelly, warning her there

was a good chance that it was a skin cancer. It was especially likely in view of her history of heavy sun exposure, and the fact that the lesion hadn't changed in response to the topical steroid creams I'd prescribed.

She seemed interested in what I told her, but hardly concerned. After all, she was only twenty-four, and she shared a common belief with most people her age—the belief that she was immortal. Besides, she had always been healthy.

As my nurse put the last piece of the dressing on the wound, I told Kelly we should have our answer within a few days. "By the way," I reminded her, "no more sun!"

"Okay, okay," she replied. "I promise I'll try!" I refused to back down despite the fact that she gave me her best scolded child look.

A week later I phoned Kelly to give her the report, and the news was mixed. The bad news was that the biopsy had revealed a locally inflammatory basal cell skin cancer. The good news was that the margins of the specimen were wide and totally free of tumor. I explained to her that we had every reason to be optimistic about the report. After all, that type of cancer is almost always cured by the excision I'd performed, and the pathologist felt we'd gotten it all. She acted slightly surprised that it had been cancerous, but she seemed oblivious to the underlying implications. I felt compelled to press the point with her.

"Kelly, you do understand what this means, don't you?"

"Sure," she replied, "it means you got all of it."

My hand flew into the air as I rolled my eyes in disbelief. "Yes, technically that's true," I said. "We did get it all . . . this time. But you really should think of this as a warning sign for you, Kelly. Your skin has been badly damaged by all the years of sun exposure and by all the time in the tanning beds. I'm concerned that if you don't stop this now, other cancers will follow, and next time it may not be cured so easily."

No response. Only tense silence. I was left to assume that my warning had not met with great appreciation, that there was a good chance we would one day be having the same talk again. I'm not usually in the business of playing prophet. In fact, when I told Kelly about the possibility of a recurrence, I hoped I would be wrong. But something deep inside told me she would be back.

Kelly had been a serious beachgoer since she was old enough to walk, and she had never slowed down. Even as an adult, she continued the sun worship. Every free weekend in the summer she traveled to her family's condo in Florida. And in the winter? Well, the invention of the tanning salon had fit nicely into her plans. It had allowed her to continue the bronzing process year-round. I didn't think she was going to give it all up so easily, even after her skin cancer. No, for some reason I wasn't sure she was convinced of the seriousness of this situation. I'll never forget what she told me just before we ended our conversation that day.

"I guess you're right. I probably should cut down on the tanning. But I love the way it makes me look, you know, so good, so . . . healthy."

Hmm, how interesting. I was just thinking to myself how it made her look sort of like a large handbag, but my thoughts aside, the facts were indisputable. As a direct result of her tanning, she was the proud owner of premature facial wrinkles, a large scar on her right forearm, and a pathology report confirming a skin cancer. Yet it made her look healthy? *I must be missing something,* I thought, but it was, after all, her decision.

A year passed before I saw Kelly again in the office. She came in for treatment of a simple sore throat, but she casually asked if I could check a mole on her leg while she was there. She said she thought it had gotten bigger, possibly even changed in color over the last few months. She wanted it removed because she didn't like the way it looked.

I examined it briefly and thought, *That makes*

two of us. The lesion in question was mostly black in color, with some scattered purple tinting. It was 1.1 centimeters in diameter, but its borders were irregular and ill defined. I feared, even then, that it might be a melanoma, the most deadly of skin cancers. I insisted we schedule a time to have it removed as soon as possible.

The next morning I once again held the scalpel over Kelly, but it was no simple shave excision. A wide and very deep incisional biopsy was necessary. Once again the interior layers of skin looked so smooth and youthful, not at all like the leathery surface tissue I'd just removed. As I was tying the knot on the last stitch, I had a sinking feeling I couldn't ignore, a feeling that Kelly's luck had just run out.

The lesion was sent out immediately, and the pathology report confirmed my fears. It was a large melanoma, and the biopsy margins revealed more tumor. More extensive surgery would be required to get it all. I called the plastic surgeon and gave him the details. I could only imagine his facial expression, but his words I remember exactly.

"Wow," he said, "what a shame . . . only twenty-five years old!"

In one sense Kelly was still a very fortunate young woman. She would survive the ordeal. From a cosmetic standpoint, however, she wasn't nearly so lucky. As I'd expected, most of her right thigh had to be removed during the operation. It was necessary to minimize the possibility that any residual cancer cells were left behind and to give her any reasonable chance for a complete cure. I spoke to her briefly after the surgery, and considering what she had been through, she seemed to be in good spirits. She stared at me with glassy eyes for several seconds, trying to shake off the effects of the anesthesia. Finally, she smiled as she recognized a familiar face among the green-clad warriors of the recovery ward.

"Thanks for coming," she told me. After she was more lucid, she revealed her new resolution. "No more sun for me, Doc, absolutely none! I've learned my lesson. I guess I should have listened to you a lot sooner, but I can assure you of one thing; I've made my last trip to the beach."

It was interesting that her most rational thoughts seemed to be drug induced, yet I believed she had learned her lesson. It had been a difficult, costly, and very painful one for her.

As I left recovery that morning, I thought how ironic it was that the very thing she thought made her look so good, so healthy, was responsible for her health problems. It had caused her to be severely disfigured physically and nearly robbed her of her life. I wondered how the myth was ever born that a deep tan is synonymous with good health—because nothing could be farther from the truth. It seems odd that we should go to such great lengths to make ourselves look more attractive on the exterior and compromise our overall health in the process. It is ridiculous to try so hard to impress and risk losing something that can never be replaced.

Kelly would testify, I believe, to the shallowness of that line of thinking. If her battle with cancer and her brush with death had taught her anything, it was that her well-being was much more important than her outward appearance. Kelly understood that it isn't that important how we look or what we appear to be to everyone else. The only thing that truly matters is the state of affairs below the skin—and whether or not we're really healthy on the inside.

Chapter 27

A PLACE IN THE HEART

He just won't talk to us at all, Doctor. All he wants to do is stay in his room, listen to that crazy, loud music on his stereo, and talk to his friends on the phone. His grades at school have gone from good to bad to worse, his attitude is horrible, and now he absolutely refuses to go anywhere with us. He won't even go to church anymore. I want something done about it right now!"

Andy pulled his faded baseball cap over his eyes, slumped down in his chair, and tried his best to ignore that he was the subject of the conversation I was having with his frustrated and very angry mother. Truthfully, it wasn't really much of a conversation. It was more of a one-sided barrage of accusations.

"Just six months ago he was making A's and B's

in school. Now he doesn't even want to *go* to school. He'll barely drag himself out of bed in the morning, and when he does make it to class, his effort is so poor. . . . There is no way he'll ever get into college now. I want him tested for drugs, for alcohol, and anything else you can test for in this office."

I knew Andy's mom desperately wanted to help him, but she was obviously doing more harm than good. I politely asked her to excuse us for a few moments so I could examine Andy alone. At first she was hesitant to do so, but finally, she agreed. Once I got her out of the room, I was able to get Andy to cooperate with me a little more.

"Andy, it appears to me that your mom is pretty upset with you. I know she was letting you have it with both barrels there for a minute, but usually, parents have their reasons when they react that way. Do you have any idea why that might be the case?"

Andy shrugged his shoulders and looked around the room. "I guess we haven't been getting along too well lately. But she nags and pesters me all the time. What you just saw was nothing compared to what I get at home. I mean . . . it's constant, you know . . . like, it never lets up! I think if she would just leave me alone, things would be much better for all of us."

"Well, I don't think that's going to happen, Andy. I think your mother loves you too much to leave you alone. You know, it sounds as though she is really concerned about the possibility you may be using some drugs. How do you feel about doing the drug testing that she asked me about?"

As you may have guessed, that was a very carefully orchestrated question. I never perform a drug test without first discussing it with the patient and obtaining his or her permission. There are several reasons for this, but the most important is based on my desire to keep the person's trust. In the long run that will prove to be much more valuable than any drug test result I could ever obtain. Besides, most of the time it isn't necessary to do the test. Any young person who is not doing drugs will be more than happy to jump at the opportunity to prove the parents wrong. On the other hand, the young person who is doing drugs will invent any number of reasons why he is physically unable to provide a specimen, or complain that so doing will cause him to compromise some great underlying moral conviction. I stood my ground and waited for Andy to choose his direction.

"Well, Doc, it's not that I mind doing the test or anything like that. I just hate to play her game, you know? I mean, I hate to make her think she won."

"I see, so you would rather not do the test, even

though it might convince your mother of your innocence."

"That's exactly right. I just don't think I should have to do it. After all, why should *she* get to make all the rules? And where does it all end? Eventually, kids everywhere will be forced to take random drug tests just because some overprotective, nosy parent wanted it. It just isn't right."

I'm sure it was just my imagination, but I could almost hear "The Star-Spangled Banner" playing in the background. As I feared, Andy was refusing the drug screen on the grounds that he was a conscientious objector. I left Andy alone for a while to reconsider his position, and I used the time to talk privately with his mother.

"Have you seen any physical evidence of drug use around your house?" I asked her. "Have you found any needles, any unusual pills, any evidence that he might be smoking pot?"

"No, Doctor, there haven't really been any obvious signs. I just know that the child living in my house now isn't the same child I've raised for the last sixteen years. Something terrible has happened to cause such a drastic change in his personality. There was a time when he enjoyed spending time with the family, doing things with his father, and playing with his younger brother. He was actively involved in the youth group at church, attending seminars, quoting Bible verses, going on weekend retreats, but all that has changed. He no longer has any interest in anything of any value."

As we were finishing our conversation, I had a deep sense of compassion for this mother. I knew she was experiencing a tremendous amount of pain as she felt her son slowly slipping away from her. But despite further discussions I had with Andy, he would not agree to have the drug screen. I told him I thought I knew why he objected so strongly, and I would be glad to arrange some help if he would accept it. He just shook his head and continued to deny everything. I knew his parents had some difficult times facing them in the next few weeks. I only hoped they could get through to their son before it was too late.

About six months later I saw Andy in the office for a routine sports physical. I was thrilled enough by the news that he was in school at all. The fact that he was trying out for the soccer team was icing on the cake. He seemed to be in exceptionally good spirits, so we talked for a longer period of time than usual. He told me he had been released from a drug treatment center about four months ago. It seems he finally confessed to using several types of narcotics, including cocaine and various prescription painkillers. The time in the rehab unit had been an eye-opening experience for him. It helped him understand the magnitude of the problem he had with the drugs, and it gave him some insight into the changes he needed to make if he was really going to turn his life around.

"You know, Doc, the amazing thing about it all is that the people who got me started *using* were some of the kids in my youth group at church. I'd go to youth rallies with them and attend all the meetings, then, when it was over, we'd drive around for a while, trying different pills to see how they would affect us. It really made me feel guilty, too, hearing all that talk about how Jesus sacrificed Himself for us. About how He died for us. Then we'd sing those songs about how much He meant to us, right before we left to start our own private party. I guess things would have been different all along if I'd really listened to the message they were teaching us. But I never paid any attention to it. I heard the stories about Jesus, but I just never let Him into my heart."

It was obvious that things were different for him now. I finished my examination and was sitting to complete his school form when he reminded me of something else.

"Don't forget, Doc, I want to do a drug screen today, too."

"Oh," I said. "I wasn't aware of that."

"Yeah, it's something I've decided I want to do about once a month. I think it will make my parents feel better. To tell you the truth, I guess it'll make me feel a little better, too. It's one of the promises I made to myself before my discharge from the center. Sort of an extra incentive to be sure things stay the way they are . . . the way they're supposed to be."

I shook Andy's hand and told him how proud I was of the progress he had made with his rehabilitation. But I thought very little about the irony of going to youth retreats and experimenting with narcotics, about hearing the message of truth, but blocking it from coming into his heart. My chance to think about what he had said came a few days later as I was talking to my own son, Christopher. I was sitting with him in his room, trying my best to get him ready for bed. As always, we were reading some of his bedtime books, singing a few songs, the usual things a boy of four wants to do to delay going to sleep.

For those of you without small children, let me explain. Only two hours before, when Christopher was destroying our home at full speed, armed terrorists wouldn't have been able to make him listen to a story or sing a song. Now, however, that was the very thing he found to be lacking to make his day complete, so we read, and we sang. We had just finished singing his favorite song, "Blue Skies and Rainbows," when he hit me with one of those questions only a child can ask. He was curious about the part of the song that says, "Jesus . . . makes His home in my heart."

"Daddy?"

"Yes, son."

"How does Jesus get into our hearts to live there? Does He just push His way in?"

I leaned over, hugged him, and told him that was a very good question.

"No, son, He really doesn't push His way into your heart. If you want Jesus to be in your heart, you have to decide to let Him in yourself."

He fell back and closed his eyes to rest just before he asked his final question for the night.

"Daddy, do you think Jesus is in my heart?"

I rubbed my hand through his hair and smiled at such a sincere question from a tired little fellow. "Yes, son, I think He is. I don't believe there's any doubt about it."

Chapter 28

A HOME FOR COLIN

It was an unusually cold and windy day for the time of year in Alabama. A day that seemed even colder because of the task I had been asked to perform. I knelt forward slowly, the knee of my best suit almost touching the wet ground, but that mattered little at the moment. Carefully, I lowered my corner of the tiny coffin to the ground and backed away with the other pall-bearers, my job completed. Five feet away from me sat two of my dearest friends on earth, Phil and Shelia, their lives forever changed by the events of the last two days.

I looked closely at my friend Phil, a strong, rugged-looking fellow with salt-and-pepper hair and broad athletic shoulders. Years ago he was a college decathlete and football star, yet he had made the transition to loving family man, weekend golfer, and successful business entrepreneur. He is the kind of guy who is liked by everyone, who never seems to make an enemy and never meets a stranger. Usually, he looked at least ten years younger than his actual age of thirty-six, but today he looked very tired. It was understandable after what he had been through. I walked over to him and put my hand on his shoulder, trying to give some comfort, but it had little effect. His tears continued to flow.

In Phil's right hand was the hand of one of the strongest and sweetest people I've ever known, his lovely wife, Shelia. She was without a doubt the best thing that ever happened to Phil, his constant source of emotional and spiritual inspiration. It was a marriage that was made in heaven. The two of them had built their wonderful life together with a lot of love, determination, and hard work. Over the last few years, Phil's company had grown into one of the most successful in the Southeast, and they were beginning to enjoy the fruits of their efforts. Anyone who looked at the family would have said they had it all: the beautiful home, two wonderful boys, and Phil's growing business. You might have been tempted to think they had the perfect life, and few people would have argued with you until suddenly and unexpectedly, they found themselves facing the midnight hour.

It was March 1992, and their younger son, Colin, had just celebrated his second birthday. They had planned to take some vacation time at the beach, but as they were packing for the trip, disaster struck the family. Little Colin had wandered into the garage and was playing quietly, so as not to be discovered. As he tried to climb through a car window, he became lodged in an awkward position and quickly suffocated. There was nothing that anyone could have done. By the time he was found, it was already too late. Shelia remembered her nursing background and performed CPR until the rescue helicopter arrived, but despite her efforts, no heartbeat or respiratory activity could be restored. Colin was flown to the local children's hospital where moments later he was pronounced dead. For Phil and Shelia, it was the end of their world. Life, at least as they had known it, was over.

I received a call from one of the nurses in the E.R. informing me of the tragedy. I could hear what she was saying, but it didn't quite seem real. I remember being literally paralyzed for a few moments during the call, thinking surely she must be wrong. I asked her to check again, possibly the identity was wrong, but no, there was no mistake. The little blond-headed fellow I had held in my arms, tossed in the air, and bounced on my knee was no longer with us. Phil and Shelia's precious little boy was gone.

Deb and I quickly arranged for a sitter and drove to be with our friends. We were stunned and speechless as we made the long trip across town. I walked slowly up the steps to the house, trying to rehearse what I would say, but my mind was totally blank.

As I entered the door, I located Phil on the sofa surrounded by other friends. He momentarily awoke from his trancelike state as he spotted me and said simply, "My baby boy is gone." I could say nothing. All I could think to do was hold him in my arms and share his tears. *What do you say? What do you do at a time like this?* I wondered. I had absolutely no answers.

Wayne Kilpatrick, an outstanding Christian minister and friend, led a touching prayer asking God for strength and understanding. His words impressed me as being well timed and well spoken. It was obvious he had asked for something we all desperately needed.

As I sat with Phil, I could hear Deb in the next room with Shelia and some of her closest friends. They were all weeping loudly, but I knew which cry belonged to Shelia. It was a haunting cry I'd heard before on several occasions, but never had I heard it more distinctly or felt it more personally.

It was the cry of a soul in pain, the cry of deep and utter despair. It was the cry of a mother who has lost her child, and believe me, there is no other sound like it on earth. It is unmistakable. And there is no appropriate consolation that will provide the mother with any relief. The only adequate response at such a time is to give compassion. That's what we were trying our best to give. It was all we had.

Even though intellectually I knew it made no sense, I couldn't help feeling a sense of guilt. I felt that if I had been there, maybe I could have done something. Maybe things would have turned out differently. It's only natural, as a physician, to think that way, but those thoughts were nonproductive. I brushed them aside for the time being.

We sat with Phil and Shelia for the rest of the day as their family began to arrive. That night proved to be a long one. Even the sedatives I prescribed were of no benefit. What little sleep my friends got that night was thoroughly intermingled with their tears.

The next morning was Sunday, and despite the situation, I still had to make rounds. I finished up at the hospital as quickly as I could, then went to be with Phil. He had an appointment to make funeral arrangements that morning, and I felt he might need my support. It wasn't until we arrived at the funeral home that I realized how right I was. There was something terribly wrong about a father planning the funeral of his son. *This just isn't right,* I thought to myself, but that's exactly what he did, and it wasn't easy. Phil fought through his tears and made those difficult decisions with greater strength than I could ever have imagined. I tried my best to ease his pain while I quietly admired his courage. With the arrangements finalized we rode home in silence, the reality of what was happening only then beginning to sink in.

I remember arriving back at Phil's house, thinking that was the most difficult thing I had ever done. And it was, until the funeral. With my partner on vacation, I was in the office seeing patients that morning. I was also scheduled to give a noon lecture about a new medication, and on such short notice I couldn't cancel. I stumbled through my talk as best I could, but my concentration wasn't what it should have been. My mind was racing ahead to the events scheduled later that day.

It was about an hour later when I arrived at the church building, and the sanctuary was already packed. I quietly took my seat near the front with the other pallbearers, dreading what was to come. It had been overcast all day, and the wind, which had been calm, was whistling in the distance.

I remember very little about the ceremony

except one song—"Jesus Loves Me," Colin's favorite song. If there was a dry eye in the building while we sang, I sure didn't see it. I tried to sing, but I couldn't seem to form the words, so I just listened. The message of the song fueled my anger and confusion, and I remember thinking that if Jesus loves us so much, how could something like this happen? But through my pain, I realized that Jesus isn't in the business of death. He is most definitely in the business of life. I remembered the question a young boy had once asked me in the E.R. about why God had taken his grandma, and I wished I'd told him that.

As the service was ending, I walked to my designated position and lifted my corner of the small casket. *This isn't the way it's supposed to be*, I thought to myself. *He's too young. There was so much life ahead of him.* But such thoughts were pointless. No argument I could create would reverse the terrible calamity. The tears I'd tried to hold back streamed down my cheeks as we turned to leave the building. It was a long walk down that aisle and an even longer ride to the cemetery.

At the graveside there were more words of wisdom designed to help put the whole thing into perspective, but in all honesty I don't remember what was said. All I remember was the rain. It started to drizzle just as Phil and Shelia were preparing to leave the graveside. I remember hugging them both again, telling them that I was sorry and that I loved them both very much. I may not have known a lot that day, but those two things I knew for sure. It was all I could think to say. I watched as they rode away and silently hoped it had been enough.

The rainfall became heavy as Deb and I made our way home that afternoon. We talked about the future and about our children. We talked about the support we knew our friends would need in the coming weeks. Neither of us knew exactly what to do. After all, how could you possibly prepare for something like that? All we knew was that we were hurting. As for Phil and Shelia, we couldn't begin to imagine the pain they felt. We only knew it was real, it was intense, and it was here to stay.

When we arrived home, we tried to explain to Lindsay and Christopher where we had been and what had happened. It was the same talk I'd had with Patrick, Colin's older brother, only the day before.

I had several long talks with Phil over the next few weeks. We played golf a few times, we had lunch, we even watched a couple of ball games on TV, but he wasn't the same. I wondered if he ever would be. Phil later told me that there was a time when he had given up the hope of ever experiencing joy again in life.

"To tell you the truth," he said, "I really didn't expect it, and what's worse, I didn't care." For Phil, life had lost its meaning. He no longer felt a purpose in his existence. His fervent prayer was that he would somehow feel a few moments' peace, but there was none to be found.

"Nighttime was the worst," he told me. That had been his special time with the boys, to wrestle, to laugh, to discuss the events of the day, just the three of them. All that was gone, and in its place was a huge void. Where there had once been such happiness, there was only emptiness. Darkness had become his enemy, his constant and painful reminder of what he had lost. He would stay awake for hours, wandering through the house alone, searching for a sense of comfort that he couldn't find.

"Even though the passing of time began to ease some of the pain, the healing process left a scar," he told me. It was a deep, painful scar on a heart that had once known such happiness.

For Shelia, things were no better. She became depressed and withdrawn. Even short trips to the store became emotional nightmares. Well-meaning friends would try to console her, and the wounds beginning to heal were easily reopened. She decided it wasn't worth it. She would rather stay home. Occasionally, she would come to church late and sit alone in the back of the building. But how could she find peace in the place where the body of her son had lain only weeks before? And her fellow Christians, though wanting to give comfort, reminded her of what she had lost.

"How are you, Shelia?" came the question from Colin's Sunday school teacher.

"Can we help in any way?" asked the father of his classmate.

Though Phil and Shelia wanted to stay close to God during that time, it became a real struggle. Shelia began to wonder, *What's the use? What's the point of trying to continue?* But during those difficult months, Shelia reached some insightful conclusions.

"I grew to realize that faith in God is an easy thing to profess when all the bills are paid, when your family is healthy, and when all is well in your life," she told me. "Yet it's a little different proposition when the rains come." And for Shelia, her calm skies had opened up into a heavy downpour.

"It was then," Shelia said, "that I began to realize my relationship with the Father wasn't just the *most important* thing in my life; it was the *one* thing I had that gave everything else meaning. After hurting and struggling for so long, I finally reached the conclusion that what mattered most on this earth was my closeness to God. For me to put my life back together again, I knew I must start with that relationship and trust Him to do the rest."

Despite the difficulty for both of them, they remained in close contact with their church family, and slowly but surely, things began to improve. At that time I, too, tried to put some things into perspective. I did some thinking about life, about family, about the future. Sure, death was an oft-encountered proposition in my line of work, but never had there been a time when I had wondered more about what it meant to me. Not to me, the doctor, but to me, the person.

I remembered going to church years ago and hearing the sermons of a great man, Edsel Burleson. As he ended each sermon, he shut his Bible, paused for a second, and proclaimed with utter determination, "I want to go to heaven." I often cringed at such a statement. Not "I hope to go to heaven," or "I've heard of a place called heaven," but "I *want* to go to heaven." I wondered how he could be so certain, yet he was. And now, for the first time in my life, faced with the realization that death comes to all, often out of season, often unexpectedly, I knew it was time for me to be sure about some things as well. I knew I had to learn from Phil and Shelia's tragedy, to grow to a greater understanding of what life and death are all about.

During the last couple of years I've tried to do that. I've continued to have my talks with Phil and Shelia, and I am happy to say that the story of these wonderful people doesn't end at the grave of their young son. A silver lining rose from behind the dark storm clouds. In the spring of 1994, Shelia gave birth to a wonderful baby girl, Madison Jane Spencer. She is truly a miracle for that family, a gift from God. And although you don't replace a child who is lost, Madison has helped them deal with the loss. She has been a real blessing to our friends and a reminder to all of us that death is not the end. We always have hope and the wonderful promise of new life.

"There are times when the pain is still intense," Shelia told me, "but it's been a lot easier to deal with now that Madison is here."

It's also been a lot easier for me since I have looked into the eyes of that precious little girl and have witnessed her beautiful smile. You see, she has helped me understand that even though I will often be unable to prolong life, there is One who creates it. Though I may not always be able to ease pain and suffering, there is One who will. And though I most certainly cannot defeat death, there is One who already has. Now that I think about it, it just doesn't seem that hard to say it anymore: I *want* to go to heaven, too.

ABOUT THE AUTHOR

David Wilhelm, M.D., is a practicing physician in Birmingham, Alabama. He combines an understanding of human nature, medical knowledge, and a warm writing style to bring human interest stories to life in a way that applies to the spiritual side of people. Dr. Wilhelm is a graduate of David Lipscomb University and the University of South Alabama College of Medicine and is board certified with the American Board of Internal Medicine.